T0311151

Easy
Bargello

25 Needlepoint Projects

Easy
Bargello

25 Needlepoint Projects

ROSEMARY DRYSDALE

THE GUILD OF MASTER CRAFTSMAN PUBLICATIONS

Contents

PROJECTS

About Bargello

I have always been a lover of all types of counted-thread embroidery and have written many books on the various techniques. The particular use of colour and pattern that is unique to Bargello makes it one of my favourites, so I am delighted that Bargello embroidery has regained popularity over the last few years.

Bargello has a long history, with samples from as far back as the thirteenth century. Some historians suggest Bargello originally took its name from a group of furnishings found in the Bargello Palace in Florence. The long, shaded patterns resemble flames, so the style became known as flame stitch or Florentine embroidery, though now Bargello is the name most often used. There are many examples to be found in museums worldwide, and many history books have interesting stories relating to the designs, folklore and associations with royalty.

Bargello is very easy to master, fairly quick to stitch and there are numerous possibilities for design and colour combinations, whether you are inspired by traditional patterns or make up your own.

The Bargello stitch is worked on a background fabric which is covered in straight stitches of various lengths. The stitches are usually worked in wool, producing a warm, heavy fabric in a relatively short period of time, which is why it became such a popular type of stitchery for covering furniture and stitching the wall hangings and tapestries that were frequently used to keep out draughts.

Today, in our centrally heated homes, Bargello is more often used decoratively than for insulation – and it can make the simplest of household objects eye-catching or add its own unique style to accessories. In this collection of projects you will find simple holiday ornaments, a bookmark, a glasses case, pillows, small purses and so much more. You can also stitch on a variety of different fabrics and use a wide range of threads to good effect.

I hope you will enjoy working this colourful counted-thread embroidery as much as I do, and that once you get hooked, you will be inspired to create your own unique and colourful patterns.

Tools and Materials

If you are an embroiderer, you probably have most of the items needed for Bargello in your stash. The fabric and threads are available at most needlework or craft stores or online, along with scissors, needles and embroidery hoops.

CANVAS

Traditionally, Bargello embroidery was worked on an even-weave canvas made from threads of linen. Canvas has an open weave, often called a 'mesh'. There are various types of canvas available, including mono canvas, interlocking canvas and Penelope canvas.

I used mono canvas for my designs as the single threads of the canvas make it less confusing when counting the stitches. Interlocking canvas is woven with fine double threads locked together to form single threads in the warp and weft, creating a firmer canvas. Penelope canvas has double threads.

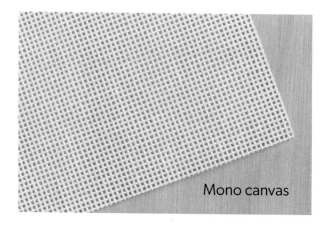

Mono canvas

Canvas comes in a variety of sizes or 'mesh' determined by the number of threads woven in the warp and the weft. A #10 canvas, or 10-count canvas, will have 10 warp threads and 10 weft threads per inch (2.5cm). A #14 canvas, or 14-count canvas, will have 14 threads per inch (2.5cm). The higher the number, the finer the canvas and the smaller the stitches. Canvas is sold in either specially cut pieces or by the yard or metre.

Canvases usually come in white or ecru, although some canvases are dyed in brighter colours. In this book I have used only white canvas.

You could also use even-weave linen or cotton fabrics, or another alternative is Aida cloth, which is usually used for embroidery but is equally suitable for Bargello. Be sure to choose a high-quality fabric with a perfectly even weave with the same number of threads per inch (2.5cm) in both the warp and weft.

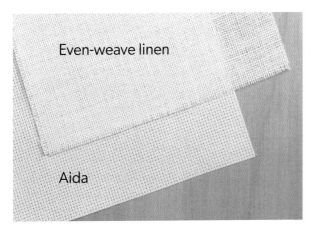

Even-weave linen

Aida

Plastic canvas
This is made of lightweight plastic with a grid of holes similar to interlocking canvas. Like fabric canvas, plastic canvas is available in different sizes, with 10-count and 14-count being the most popular. It's available both as clear and in bright colours, and can be bought in sheets and a variety of cut-out shapes, such as ovals, circles, hearts and stars. The advantage of using plastic canvas is that it can be cut into different shapes, it doesn't fray and it is very sturdy, making it a good choice for items like plant holders, boxes and coasters.

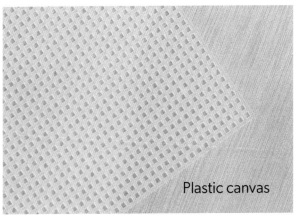

Plastic canvas

PRE-MADE ITEMS
Some of the projects use ready-made kits, which make a good introduction to Bargello. If you purchase from a different manufacturer than the one shown in the project, you may find the size varies slightly.

NEEDLES

Tapestry needles

Tapestry needles are used for Bargello. A tapestry needle has an elongated eye, a thin body and a blunt point. Needles are identified according to numbers: the higher the number, the finer the needle. It is important that the right size needle be chosen for the correct canvas or fabric count. For example, a 14-count canvas uses a #20 needle and a 10-count canvas uses a larger #18 needle.

The size of the eye of the needle must be large enough to allow the thread to slide evenly through, but not too small that it causes the thread to fray or makes it difficult to thread. Too large a needle can make it a problem to pass between the canvas or fabric threads and will end up pushing them out of shape. It is a good idea to have a selection of needle sizes on hand so you can match the correct needle with the project.

Sewing needles

You will also need some sewing needles for tacking (basting) and finishing projects.

SCISSORS

Embroidery scissors

A pair of well-made embroidery scissors with sharp points and fine, tempered blades are essential to have on hand. They should be kept in a scissor case to avoid damaging the points. (If you don't have one, the project on page 118 could be a good one to start with.)

Fabric scissors

You will also need a large pair of sharp fabric scissors to cut your canvas or fabric. Do not use any of your scissors for cutting anything other than threads or fabrics as they can be easily blunted.

YARNS AND THREADS

If you love colour, you will love working Bargello patterns. Embroidery yarns and threads come in hundreds of different colours and shades, so the possibilities for colouring designs are endless.

Originally Bargello was worked in a tightly woven wool yarn for its long-lasting and insulating properties. I have used a variety of yarns and threads in this book, including tapestry wool, Persian wool, matt cotton thread, six-strand embroidery thread, or floss, and pearl cotton.

Tapestry wool

A soft, twisted 4-ply yarn made from 100% wool, tapestry wool is used as a single strand and is only suitable for 10-count or 14-count canvas. It is sold in many colours in small skeins of about 8¾ yards (8 metres) per skein. It can be found in speciality needlework stores and online.

Although tapestry wool resembles knitting yarn, do not substitute knitting yarn for your Bargello embroidery as in most cases it does not wear well, it can pill and it twists easily during stitching.

Persian wool

Unlike tapestry wool, Persian wool is a 3-ply yarn with a tight twist that can be separated into three individual strands. The advantage of the three separate strands is that all three strands held together work well for 10-count canvas and two strands held together work for 14-count canvas. One strand is rarely used but would work for a very fine canvas, such as 20-count.

Matt cotton

This cotton has a matt finish because it is not mercerized – a chemical treatment that makes threads take up dyes and other finishes more readily – and this 'softens' the appearance of the colours. It comes in a single strand and in small skeins and is non-divisible.

Embroidery thread or floss

Also with a brilliant sheen and sold in small skeins, embroidery thread, or floss, is made up of six individual strands twisted together. These can be separated and used as two, three, four, five or six strands, depending on which gives the best coverage, so it works on a variety of canvas or thread counts. This is the most popular embroidery thread and is available in hundreds of colours.

Pearl cotton

Also a single, non-divisible strand that comes in a twisted skein or ball, pearl cotton has a beautiful lustre due to the mercerization process. It comes in sizes #3, #5 and #8 – the higher the number, the finer the thread.

Sewing thread

This is used for tacking (basting) and finishing projects.

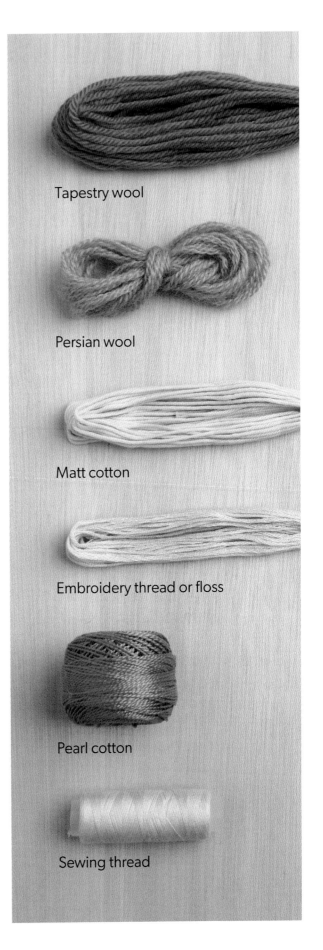

Tapestry wool

Persian wool

Matt cotton

Embroidery thread or floss

Pearl cotton

Sewing thread

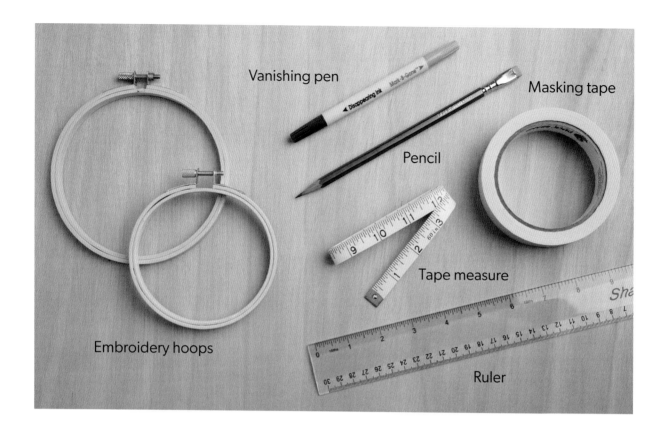

Vanishing pen

Masking tape

Pencil

Tape measure

Embroidery hoops

Ruler

OTHER EQUIPMENT

You will find a few other pieces of equipment useful but not essential.

Embroidery hoops

Different-sized hoops can be used to hold fabric in place and keep it taut for stitching. This works best for non-canvas fabrics. The hoop can also be used to frame your finished stitching.

Masking tape

Masking tape is necessary for sealing the edges of the canvas to prevent them from fraying.

Ruler or tape measure

You'll need a tape measure to mark out the stitching area for some of the larger projects. You may find a ruler easier to work with for the smaller projects.

A NOTE ON MEASUREMENTS

The measurements are given in imperial and metric, so choose one system and stick with it. The conversions have been rounded to give convenient lengths whichever system you choose.

Pencil or vanishing pen

Some people use a pencil or vanishing pen to mark the area to be embroidered instead of tacking (basting).

Iron and ironing board

Most projects recommend pressing the finished piece on an ironing board or an appropriate padded surface.

Bargello Basics

Let's look at the principles of this fascinating embroidery technique.

ESSENTIAL PRINCIPLES

The relationship between thread and fabric is very important in Bargello work as the stitches must cover the canvas or fabric background with very little, if any, canvas or fabric showing through. I have indicated the canvas, yarn and needle size needed for each project to get the best results. When experimenting on your own designs, be sure that the needle and yarn pull through the background fabric easily, that the stitches lie flat and that all the background fabric is covered as much as possible by the stitches.

Always make sure that any type of yarn or thread you are working with is of the finest quality and colourfast, as some of your Bargello pieces may need laundering.

To summarize, there are three conceptual points to note.

• Buy the best quality fabric and yarns that are available.

• Use the correct weight of yarn for the background fabric.

• Use the correct size needle to accommodate the yarn and still be fine enough to slip between the fabric threads.

CHOOSING COLOURS

In the instructions for each project, I recommend how much thread or yarn you'll need. The length used is approximate, as variations exist in how much thread or yarn is left at the beginning and end of each length. It is always a good idea to purchase some extra skeins.

All the threads used have colour numbers. If a colour is not available, choose as close a shade as possible, or select your own colour palette. Use other sources for inspiration – there are many examples of great colour combinations in magazines, stores or online.

Bargello Stitches

You can use a variety of embroidery stitches on your Bargello projects. Also included here are the ordinary sewing stitches you need to complete your projects. Do not pull stitches too tightly or they will distort the canvas threads.

EMBROIDERY STITCHES
Gobelin stitch

Bargello embroidery is based on a simple upright stitch worked in a straight line, called Gobelin stitch. It is usually worked over a stated number of canvas threads, usually 2, 3, 4 or 6, and once the length of stitch is established, all the stitches are worked at the same length.

Come up at A, go down at B and come up at C. The length of the stitches will vary when you work compensating stitches (page 15), which are used to fill in any canvas areas remaining uncovered at the top and the bottom of the pattern.

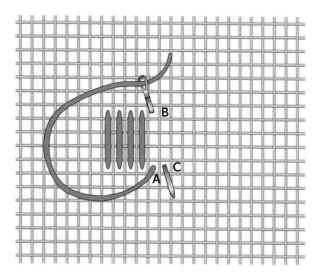

Zigzag Gobelin stitch

To create this zigzag stitch, also called Florentine stitch, you work the straight stitches over the set number of canvas threads (usually 4 threads) in steps. To create steps, stitches are placed next to each other but move either up or down by one or more canvas threads. The pattern moves up to form peaks or down to form valleys.

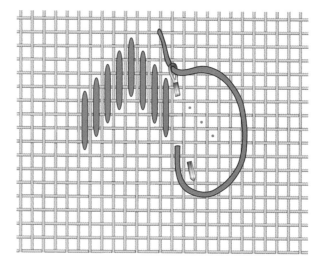

To work the second row, change the yarn or thread colour and begin stitching. Wherever possible, bring the needle up at the bottom of the stitch through an empty hole and insert it back down through the hole used by the stitch in the previous row. This is important when working subsequent rows because when pushing the needle down, rather than up, it is easier to avoid splitting the yarn of the previous row.

Stitches can also be worked in blocks of two, three or more stitches, ultimately making the steps wider.

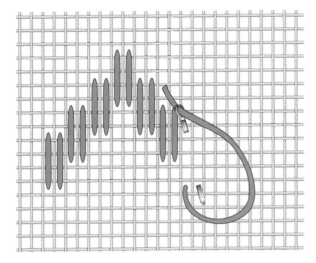

Varying the width of the blocks of the steps creates an arc, which can also be used to make circles and other rounded shapes. Groups of stitches help to soften the curve.

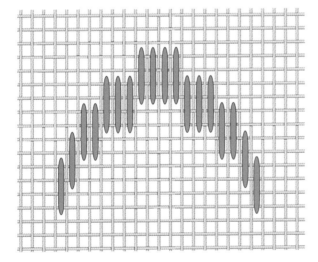

Compensating stitches

Compensating stitches are used to fill in canvas threads to make a straight edge at the top and bottom of the design, and sometimes at the sides. Some of these stitches are shorter lengths and fill out the pattern so all the canvas is covered. You will see that some charts (for example on page 26) show all the full repeats of the pattern, and a space going right up to the edge. This helps you to see the shape and structure of the pattern. To fill this space, carry on with your stitching, missing out parts of each row that would be beyond the tacking (basting) that marks the edge of the piece, working compensating stitches where there is not room for a full-length stitch.

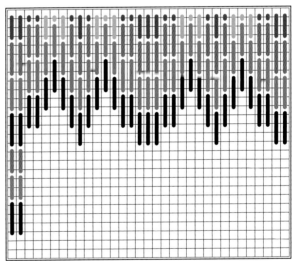

- ▬ Black
- ▬ Blue
- ▬ Red
- ▬ Black compensating stitch
- ▬ Red compensating stitch

SEWING STITCHES

Tacking (basting) or running stitch

Tacking holds two or more pieces of fabric together while you sew. It is also used to mark the starting point for your embroidery. Working from right to left, bring the needle up at A, down at B and up at C. Continue, spacing the stitches evenly.

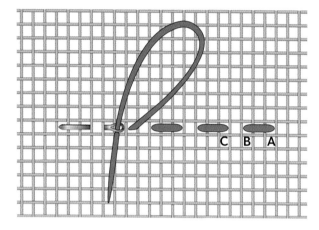

Backstitch

Backstitch is used to sew two pieces of fabric together. Working from right to left, bring the needle up at A, make a small backwards stitch by going down at B, then bring the needle up at C. Continue, bringing the needle up a stitch length ahead and down into the hole made by the last stitch.

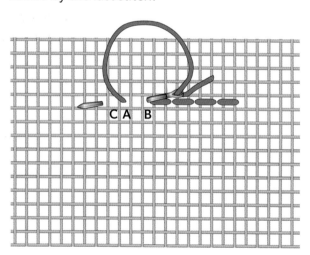

Overcast stitch

Overcasting creates a finished edge on canvas projects. When the embroidery is finished, fold the remaining canvas to the wrong side. You will get a sharper edge if you try to have a thread of the canvas on the fold, as shown. Begin stitching and work over the stated number of canvas threads, over the fold to the wrong side, and to the front in the next canvas hole. Bring your needle to the front at point A, then bring it through to the front again at B. Continue until the edge is covered. Trim off any excess canvas.

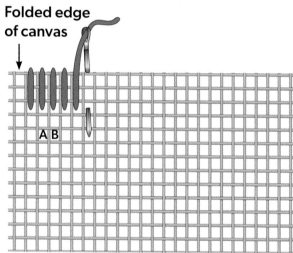

Folded edge of canvas

Slip stitch

This is the basic sewing stitch used to invisibly sew two pieces of fabric together. Catch a thread from under the fabric with a needle; at the same time catch a single thread on the fold of the fabric. Repeat, keeping the stitches as even as possible.

Other techniques

Read this section before you make a start on any of the projects and you should find the instructions straightforward to follow.

BEGINNING YOUR PROJECTS

Preparing the canvas

If you are using canvas, cut it to the size listed in the instructions.

Tape around the four sides with masking tape. To do this, simply press half the width of the tape along one edge of the canvas, then fold the remaining tape to the wrong side. Trim the ends and press to seal. Repeat on the remaining edges.

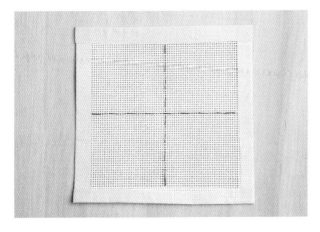

If you are using a fabric that frays, overcast round the edge or fold over the edge then tack (baste) to create a single-fold hem around the edge. Your stitches do not have to be close together.

Linen fabric

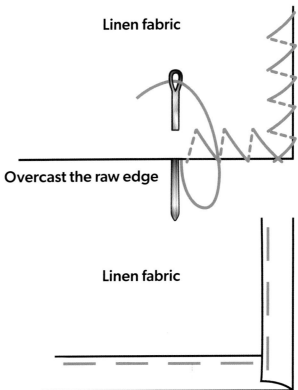

Overcast the raw edge

Linen fabric

Turn over a single hem and tack (baste)

Using a hoop

If you are working a design in a hoop, insert the tacking (basting) before you place the fabric in the hoop. Unscrew the hoop and place the fabric centrally over the smaller hoop. Carefully place the larger hoop on top and press it down, easing out any wrinkles. Tighten the hoop slightly, then pull the fabric taut before tightening the screw firmly.

Marking the canvas

When instructed, tack (baste) lines horizontally and vertically using a sewing thread to mark the middle. If you are working a mitred pattern, also tack diagonal lines. Then outline the exact dimensions of the Bargello area you are working on. The dimensions given in the projects are the number of stitches wide and the number of threads worked over tall.

Preparing embroidery thread

When working with six-strand embroidery thread, it's best to separate the strands one by one, then put them back together before threading them through the needle. This creates a fuller and very even Bargello stitch.

To separate the strands, cut an 18–20in (46–50cm) length of thread from the skein. This is the perfect length; if you make it any longer, it is likely to tangle and knot.

Hold the strands at the top, then pull the threads out one by one, pulling them upwards to avoid tangling. Then place the threads back together, side by side, before threading the needle.

Using pearl cotton

Pearl cotton, unlike embroidery thread, does not have to be separated but is used as a single strand. To cut the pearl cotton skeins into 18in (46cm) strands, slip both labels to the middle of the skein; do not remove the labels. At one end of the skein there will be two loops. Cut across the middle of each loop. This will give you a number of 18in (46cm) lengths of pearl cotton. Remove one strand at a time by pulling it out from the middle of the skein.

FOLLOWING THE CHARTS

Refer to the chart to work the pattern and colour sequence. If you start in the middle of the piece, stitch half the row and return to the middle point, then work the other end of the row as a mirror image. You can use a post-it note or mark off on a photocopy of the first chart if it helps you to follow the pattern. If you start at the arrow, follow the first row, then you can work in either direction.

To make them easy to follow, the charts show the same colours used in the embroidery, with the exception of projects using white, which would be difficult to distinguish from the canvas. White stitches are therefore indicated by a light grey to ensure clarity when stitching the projects.

The foundation row

Once you have everything prepared, you can start your embroidery.

Where the vertical and horizontal tacking (basting) stitches cross in the middle or the corner, or where the arrow is indicated on the chart, is the starting point for the first row of stitching. This row establishes the pattern.

Cut a piece of yarn about 18in (46cm) long, knot one end and thread the other through the needle. Take the needle down through the front of the fabric at A, away from your starting point in the direction of your first stitch, then up at the starting point B. The thread will be stitched over and held in place as you start to stitch. When you reach the knot, be sure the thread is covered on the wrong side. Cut off the knot.

This is called an away knot and it can be used when sewing in a straight line.

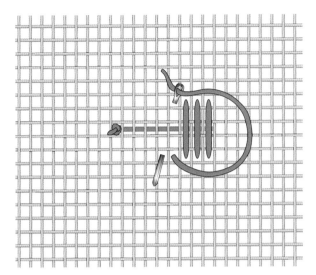

However, most Bargello stitches are worked diagonally, so the away knot is placed on the diagonal.

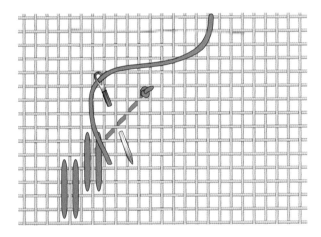

Changing the thread

When you are running out of yarn or thread in your needle, take the needle to the wrong side of the work and run it under about four to six stitches on the wrong side to secure it. Trim off any excess thread.

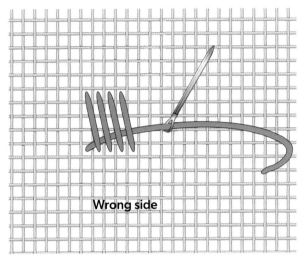

Wrong side

To begin a new strand, use an away knot or run the new yarn or thread under several stitches to secure it, then begin stitching.

Projects

Bargello Heart Pocket

SKILL LEVEL – INTERMEDIATE

A simple stitched square easily converts to an attractive and handy pocket when sewn onto a plain bag, but you could also sew it onto a jacket, jeans or any item of clothing.

YOU'LL NEED

FABRIC

- 14in (36cm) square soft fabric bag
- 10in (25cm) square 18-count white mono canvas
- 10in (25cm) square white cotton for lining

THREADS

- Matt cotton thread
  (shown in DMC Retors mat cotton)
  Two skeins of each
      Very dark blue #2824
      Medium blue #2826
  One skein of each
      Light blue #2800
      Dark yellow #2727
      Light yellow #2745
      White #Blanc
- Sewing thread

HABERDASHERY

- Masking tape
- Tapestry needle #22
- Sewing needle or sewing machine
- Scissors

STITCHES USED

(pages 14–16)
- Zigzag Gobelin stitch
- Compensating stitches
- Tacking (basting) stitch
- Overcast stitch
- Slip stitch

PREPARATION

(pages 17–18)
- Tape the edges of the canvas using masking tape
- Tack (baste) a line 121 threads wide × 114 threads high (about 6½in [16.5cm] square) to mark the stitching area
- Tack to mark the centre

FINISHED SIZE

6½in (16.5cm) square

METHOD

Using 1 strand of very dark blue mat cotton, each stitch is worked over the canvas by referring to the chart. Start at the stitches indicated by the arrow. Each stitch is worked over 4 canvas threads, side by side, stepping up or down 2 fabric threads. Work all the dark blue outlines first. Then fill in the remaining colours following the chart for the colour sequence. Ignore the row marked "overcast stitches" on the chart at this stage.

Work compensating stitches at the top and bottom of the piece to fill in the canvas for a straight edge.

Fold the upper edge of the canvas to the wrong side, leaving 2 rows of empty canvas threads at the top. Work a row of overcast stitches using dark blue through both layers.

FINISHING

Remove the tacking (basting) threads. Trim the canvas to ½in (1.25cm) from the stitching. Place the right side of the lining fabric and the right side of the stitched piece together. Tack around the 2 sides and lower edge. Machine stitch or use tiny backstitches to sew around the 3 sides. Remove the tacking thread and trim the backing fabric to the same size as the canvas. Trim across the lower corners. Turn to the right side and square out the corners. Fold the top edge of the lining to the inside below the overcast stitching and sew in place. Press lightly on the wrong side on a padded surface.

Centre the pocket on the bag and tack in place. Hand sew the pocket to the bag on 3 sides using small, neat stitches.

BARGELLO HEART POCKET CHART

Please note split charts overlap in the centre

OVERCAST STITCHES

CENTRE

BEGIN HERE →

CENTRE →

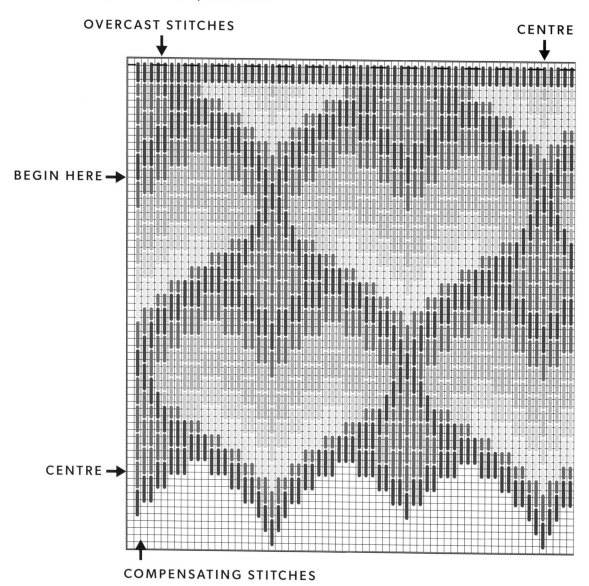

COMPENSATING STITCHES

KEY

- ■ Very dark blue #2824
- ■ Medium blue #2826
- ■ Light blue #2800
- ■ Dark yellow #2727
- ■ Light yellow #2745
- ■ White #Blanc

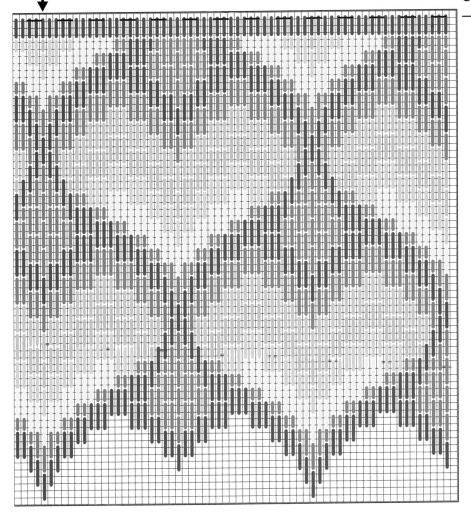

REPEAT VERTICALLY TO MATCH THE DIAGRAM BELOW

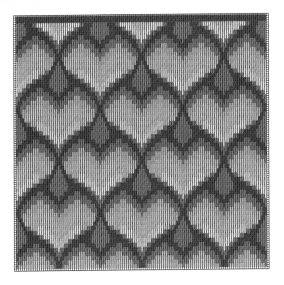

No.232

No.219

Credit Card Wallet

SKILL LEVEL – EASY

As we use cash less and less, having a case for carrying cards becomes increasingly essential. Pretty diamond patterning on a pre-finished purse makes this quick to stitch.

YOU'LL NEED

FABRIC

- Pre-finished stitch and zip coin purse (see Resources, page 138)

THREADS

- Pearl cotton #3
  (shown in DMC pearl cotton #3)
  One skein of each
  > Dark blue #796
  > Medium blue #798
  > Pale blue #809
  > Pink #223
- Sewing thread

HABERDASHERY

- Tapestry needle #22
- Sewing needle or sewing machine
- Scissors

STITCHES USED

(pages 14–16)
- Zigzag Gobelin stitch
- Compensating stitches
- Tacking (basting) stitch

PREPARATION

(pages 17–18)
- Read the instructions from the manufacturer before beginning stitching
- Tack (baste) the vertical centre of the wallet

FINISHED SIZE

4½ × 3in (11.5 × 7.5cm)

METHOD

Begin stitching using the pearl cotton #3 on the left side, 13 threads down from the top. Work the first zigzag row in dark blue, following the chart and colour key, working from the centre out to each side. This is the foundation row. Each stitch is worked side by side over 4 canvas threads in steps, each stepping up or down over 2 threads. Each subsequent row is worked in the same way in the colours indicated.

Work compensating stitches at the top and bottom of the piece to fill in for a straight edge.

FINISHING

Follow the finishing instructions from the manufacturer.

CREDIT CARD WALLET CHART

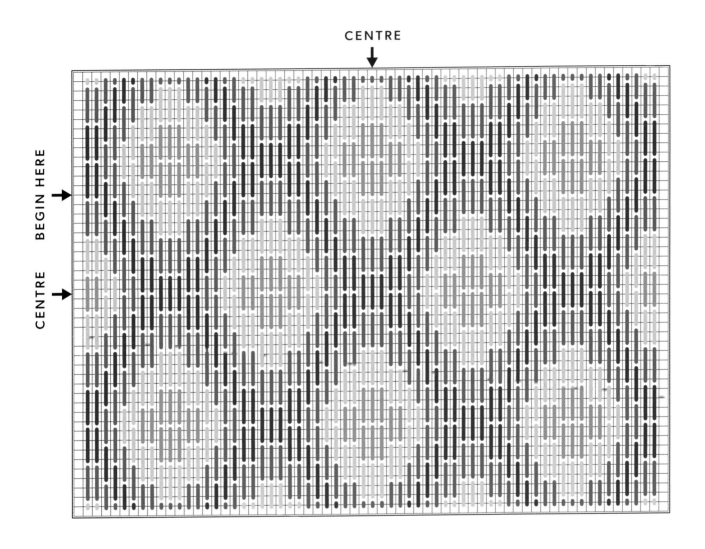

CENTRE

BEGIN HERE

CENTRE

KEY

█ Dark blue #796

█ Medium blue #798

█ Pale blue #809

█ Pink #223

Diamond Pattern Hand Towel

SKILL LEVEL – EASY

The towel used here has an Aida strip woven in, so after stitching it requires no finishing. Alternatively, you could embroider a piece of Aida, then sew it to an ordinary towel. Customize the colours to match your bathroom.

YOU'LL NEED

FABRIC
- Velour guest towel with Aida panel (see Resources, page 138)

THREADS
- Six-strand embroidery thread (shown in DMC stranded cotton)
  One skein of each
  Dark blue #799
  Medium blue #800
  Light blue #3756
  Dark green #904
  Medium green #3347
  Light green #772
- Sewing thread

HABERDASHERY
- Tapestry needle #22
- Sewing needle
- Scissors

STITCHES USED
(pages 14–16)
- Zigzag Gobelin stitch
- Tacking (basting) stitch

PREPARATION
(pages 17–18)
- Tack (baste) the Aida band to mark the centre

FINISHED SIZE
Towel is 12 × 19½in (30 × 49.5cm)

METHOD

Begin stitching at the centre, 3 Aida squares down from the top of the Aida band with dark blue thread, following the chart. Work from the centre out to each side. Work the dark blue diamond outlines first, then fill in the centre sections. Each stitch is worked over 4 Aida squares, side by side, stepping up and down 2 Aida squares in groups of 1, 2 and 3. Follow the chart for the colour sequence.

FINISHING

Remove the tacking (basting) stitches. Lightly press the wrong side on a padded surface.

DIAMOND PATTERN HAND TOWEL CHART

Please note split charts overlap in the centre

CENTRE/BEGIN HERE

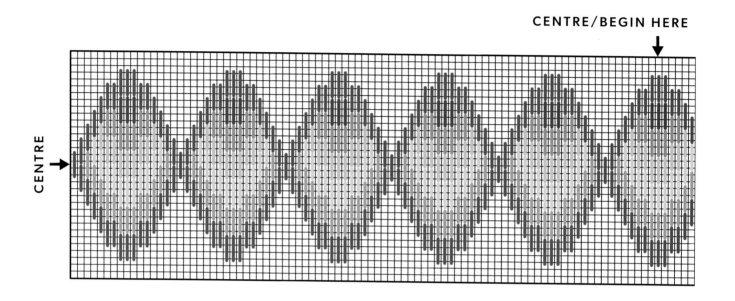

CENTRE

KEY

Dark blue #799

Medium blue #800

Light blue #3756

Dark green #904

Medium green #3347

Light green #772

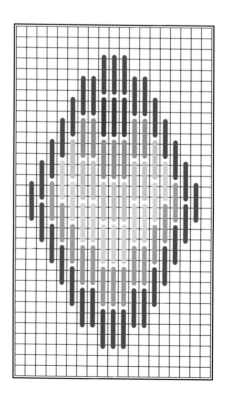

CENTRE/BEGIN HERE

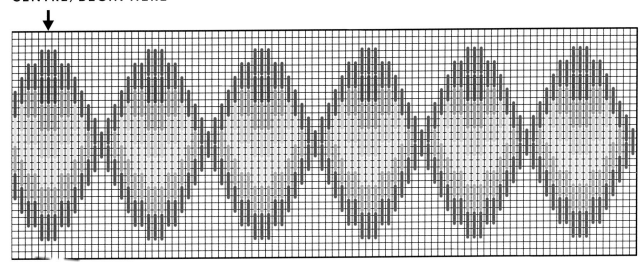

Four-Way Decorative Hoop

SKILL LEVEL – INTERMEDIATE

Working Bargello in four directions allows a designer to create mirror images of a motif. Much easier than it looks, one motif is finished, then the fabric is turned 45 degrees, and the motif is repeated.

YOU'LL NEED

FABRIC
- 9in (23cm) square 18-count white even-weave linen
- 4¼in (11cm) diameter circle white felt for backing

THREADS
- Six-strand embroidery thread (shown in DMC stranded cotton)
  One skein of each
  - Dark blue #824
  - Purple #208
  - Dark turquoise #943
  - Medium turquoise #913
  - Light turquoise #964
  - Light green #564
- Thread for finishing back of hoop: white pearl cotton #5
- Sewing thread

HABERDASHERY
- 5in (13cm) embroidery hoop
- Tapestry needle #22
- Embroidery needle #6
- Sewing needle
- Scissors

STITCHES USED
(pages 14–16)
- Zigzag Gobelin stitch
- Tacking (basting) stitch

PREPARATION
(pages 17–18)
- Tack (baste) both straight and diagonally to mark the centre of the fabric, tacking the lines over 2 fabric threads. The diagonal lines are the mitre lines necessary for a 4-way design. They must be stitched accurately so the quarters match up
- Centre the fabric in the hoop, assembling it securely

FINISHED SIZE
5in (13cm) diameter

METHOD

Using 6 strands of thread, each stitch is worked over the fabric by referring to the chart. Work on one diamond at a time. Start at the centre of the piece, so the bottom of the first diamond, using dark blue. Each stitch is worked over 4 canvas threads side by side, and 4 threads tall. Follow the chart for the colour sequence. When 1 diamond is complete, turn the hoop so that the next diamond is vertical. Work all 4 units.

FINISHING

Remove the tacking (basting) stitches. Trim the fabric to a circle, leaving at least 2in (5cm) of fabric beyond the hoop. With a long length of pearl cotton #5 and the wrong side facing, insert the embroidery needle into the fabric ½in (1.25cm) from the outer edge of the hoop. Secure with several double stitches, then work a circle of running stitches around the perimeter of the hoop, leaving a long tail.

Trim any excess fabric at least ½in (1.25cm) from the running stitches. Gather the running stitches by pulling the pearl cotton until the fabric fits snugly around the inner hoop. Secure the thread. Place the felt backing on top of the fabric and, using pearl cotton, stitch through both felt and fabric layers to attach the backing.

FOUR-WAY DECORATIVE HOOP CHART

CENTRE

CENTRE

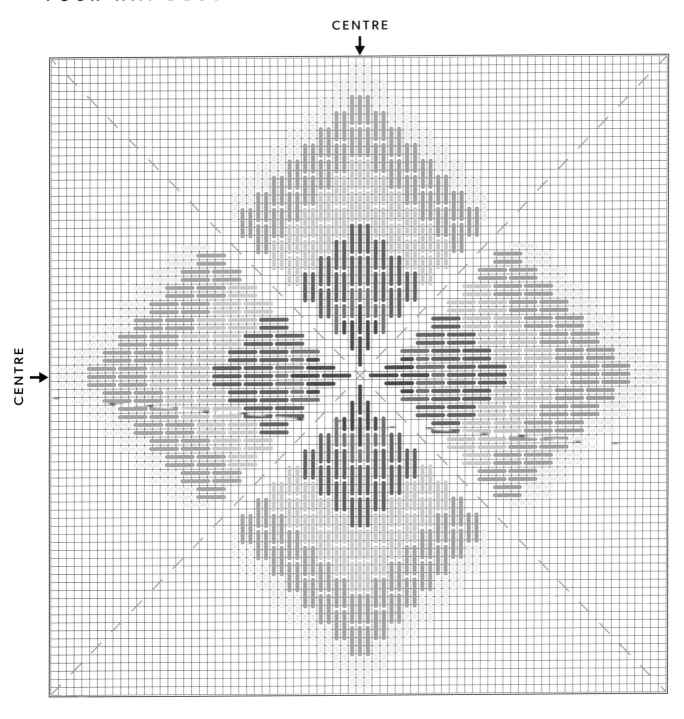

KEY

■ Dark blue #824		▨ Light turquoise #964	
▨ Purple #208		░ Light green #564	
▨ Dark turquoise #943		– – Tacking (basting) lines	
▨ Medium turquoise #913			

Boho Wall Hanging

SKILL LEVEL – EASY

This tasselled Boho-style wall hanging features a traditional zigzag pattern often used in the 18th century to upholster chair seats and backs. Felt makes finishing the back quick and easy.

YOU'LL NEED

FABRIC
- 12½ × 16½in (32 × 42cm) piece 14-count white mono canvas
- 8½ × 12½in (21.5 × 32cm) piece white felt for backing

THREADS
- Pearl cotton #3
  (shown in DMC pearl cotton #3)
  One skein of each
  - Terracotta #918
  - Dark peach #922
  - Pink #353
  - Medium peach #402
  - Ecru #739
  - Light brown #407
  - Medium green #320
  - Dark green #501
- Six-strand embroidery thread
  (shown in DMC stranded cotton)
  Two skeins
  - Terracotta #918
- Sewing thread

HABERDASHERY
- Masking tape
- Tapestry needle #20
- Sewing needle or sewing machine
- Scissors
- ¼in (65mm) dowel, 11in (28cm) long
- 24in (61cm) decorative twisted cord for the hanger

STITCHES USED
(pages 14–16)
- Zigzag Gobelin stitch
- Compensating stitches
- Tacking (basting) stitch

PREPARATION
(pages 17–18)
- Tape the edges of the canvas using masking tape
- Tack (baste) an 8½ × 12½in (21.5 × 32cm) rectangle to mark the stitching area
- Tack to mark the centre

FINISHED SIZE
8½ × 12½in (21.5 × 32cm)

METHOD

Using 1 strand of cotton, each stitch is worked over the canvas by referring to the chart. Start at the dark green stitches indicated by the arrow, 4 threads below the tacking (basting) line. This is the foundation row. Each stitch is worked over 4 canvas threads side by side, stepping up or down 2 fabric threads. Follow the chart for the colour sequence.

Work compensating stitches at the top and bottom of the piece to fill in for a straight edge.

FINISHING

Remove the tacking (basting) threads. Press lightly on the wrong side on a padded surface. Trim the canvas to ½in (1.25cm) on the sides and lower edge. Trim to 1½in (4cm) at the top edge for the fold. Fold the canvas on the sides and lower edge to the wrong side and tack, mitring the corners. Hand sew in place with slip stitches.

To make the rod pocket, fold the top of the canvas to the wrong side, mitring the corners. Tack in place, leaving an opening for the dowel to slip though. Hand sew in place.

TASSELS

Make a tassel from one end of the skein of embroidery thread.

1 Cut 4 × 12in (30cm) lengths of embroidery thread from one skein; keep the second skein intact. Thread one strand of cut embroidery thread through the loop at the top of the skein. Make a double knot to secure.

2 Take the second strand of cut thread and wrap it around the top of the skein. Tie securely. Using a needle, hide the ends of this thread by pushing the needle into the wrap and pointing it downwards into the middle of the skein.

3 Slide the label down 3in (7.5cm) from the top. Cut above the label. Repeat for the other end of the skein.

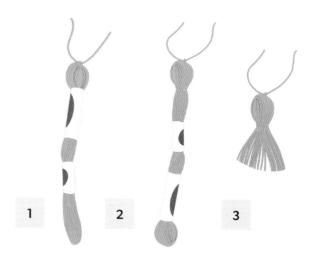

Insert the dowel into the opening and centre it. Tie the tassels to the dowel and slip the remaining thread into the rod pocket.

To secure the ends of the cord so they do not unravel, with needle and thread, sew the twists together 1½in (4cm) from each end. Gently untwist the cord above the sewing and insert the dowel. Slip the remaining ends of the cord into the rod pocket and stitch to secure.

BOHO WALL HANGING CHART

COMPENSATING STITCHES

BEGIN HERE

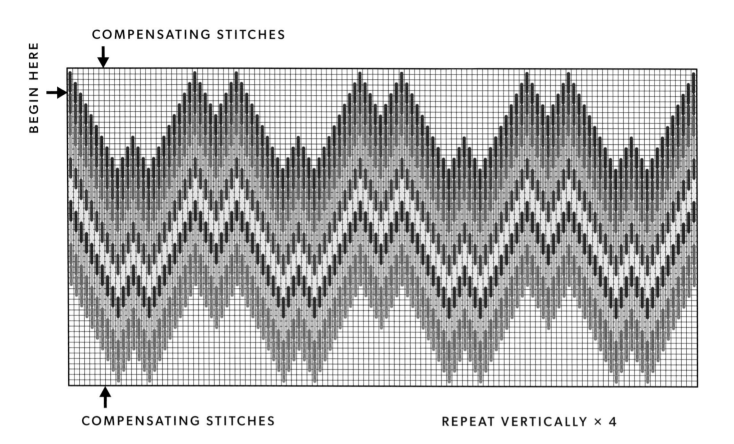

COMPENSATING STITCHES

REPEAT VERTICALLY × 4

KEY

Terracotta #918

Dark peach #922

Pink #353

Medium peach #402

Ecru #739

Light brown #407

Medium green #320

Dark green #501

CENTRE

Green Door Hanger

This design begins as a square, then the edges are folded, envelope style, to form a diamond. Adding a hanger and tassel allows this to be hung on a door handle, dresser drawer pull or on a wall hook.

YOU'LL NEED

FABRIC
- 8in (20cm) square 18-count white mono canvas

THREADS
- Pearl cotton #5
  (shown in DMC pearl cotton #5)
  One skein of each
  - Dark green #991
  - Medium green #993
  - Light green #955
  - Pale green #504
- Six-strand embroidery thread
  (shown in DMC stranded cotton)
  One skein
  - Medium green #993
- Sewing thread

HABERDASHERY
- Masking tape
- Tapestry needle #22
- Sewing needle
- Small amount of fibrefill for stuffing
- Scissors
- 9in (23cm) green rat tail cord

STITCHES USED
(pages 14–16)
- Zigzag Gobelin stitch
- Compensating stitches
- Tacking (basting) stitch
- Overcast stitch
- Slip stitch

PREPARATION
(pages 17–18)
- Tape the edges of the canvas using masking tape
- Tack (baste) a line 77 threads wide × 78 threads high (about 4in [10cm] square) to mark the stitching area
- Tack to mark the centre

FINISHED SIZE
4in (10cm) square

METHOD

Using 1 strand of pearl cotton #5, each stitch is worked over the canvas by referring to the chart. Start the stitches at the top centre using dark green and work to each side. Each stitch is worked over 4 canvas threads, side by side. This is the foundation row. Follow the chart for the colour sequence, working the following rows from either side.

Work compensating stitches at the top and bottom of the piece to fill in for a straight edge.

FINISHING

Remove the tacking (basting) threads. Press lightly on the wrong side on a padded surface. Trim the canvas to ½in (1.25cm) from the stitching.

Fold the raw canvas to the wrong side on all 4 sides, mitring the corners. Tack in place. With the wrong side facing, fold all 4 corners to meet in the centre. Using 2 strands of embroidery thread and overcast stitch, sew the edges together from the centre out to the corners, leaving half the seam open on the final seam. Insert the stuffing. Fold the cord in half, and sew to the 4th corner, then sew the remaining seam closed with slip stitches.

TASSEL

Make a tassel from one end of the skein of embroidery thread.

1 Cut 2 × 12in (30cm) lengths of embroidery thread and thread one strand of cut embroidery thread through the loop at the top of the skein. Make a double knot to secure.

2 Take the second strand of cut thread and wrap around the top of the skein. Tie securely. Using a needle, hide the ends of this thread by pushing the needle into the wrap and pointing it downwards into the middle of the skein.

3 Slide the label down 3in (7.5cm) from the top. Cut above the label.

Sew the tassel to the lower corner.

GREEN DOOR HANGER CHART

CENTRE/BEGIN HERE

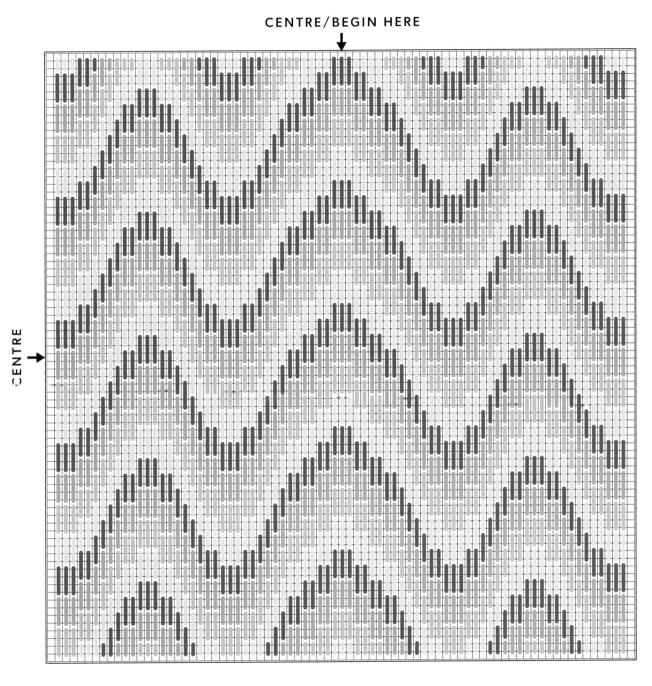

KEY

■ Dark green #991

■ Medium green #993

■ Light green #955

■ Pale green #504

The Hamptons' Tile Pillow

SKILL LEVEL – EXPERIENCED

Featuring the cool blues so popular in the seaside communities of The Hamptons on Long Island, New York, this stunning throw pillow is also reminscent of a Turkish tile design. Plush velvet finishes the back.

YOU'LL NEED

FABRIC

- 13 × 18in (33 × 46cm) piece 14-count white mono canvas
- 13 × 18in (33 × 46cm) piece turquoise velvet for backing

THREADS

- Tapestry wool
  (shown in DMC tapestry wool)
  Eight skeins
      White #Blanc
  Seven skeins
      Dark turquoise #7596
  Four skeins
      Light turquoise #7598
- Sewing thread

HABERDASHERY

- Masking tape
- Tapestry needle #20
- Sewing needle or sewing machine
- Scissors
- Fibrefill or pillow form

STITCHES USED

(pages 14–16)
- Zigzag Gobelin stitch
- Compensating stitches
- Tacking (basting) stitch
- Backstitch
- Slip stitch

PREPARATION

(pages 17–18)
- Tape the edges of the canvas using masking tape
- Tack (baste) a line to make a 9 × 13½in (23 × 34cm) rectangle to mark the stitching area
- Tack to mark the centre

FINISHED SIZE

9 × 13½in (23 × 34cm)

METHOD

Using 1 strand of wool, each stitch is worked over the canvas by referring to the chart. Start at the dark turquoise stitches indicated by the arrow on the left side, 20 threads down from the tacking (basting) line. Work all the dark turquoise tile outlines first, then fill the centres following the chart.

Work compensating stitches at the top and bottom of the piece to fill in for a straight edge.

FINISHING

Remove the tacking (basting) threads. Press lightly on the wrong side on a padded surface. Trim the canvas to ½in (1.25cm) from the stitching.

Place the right side of the backing fabric and the right side of the stitched piece together. Tack around all sides. Machine stitch or use tiny backstitches to sew around 3 sides and 1in (2.5cm) in from each side on the bottom side. Remove the tacking thread and trim the backing fabric to the same size as the canvas. Trim across the corners. Turn to the right side, square out the corners; insert the pillow form or stuffing and hand sew the opening closed with slip stitches.

THE HAMPTONS' TILE PILLOW CHART

COMPENSATING STITCHES

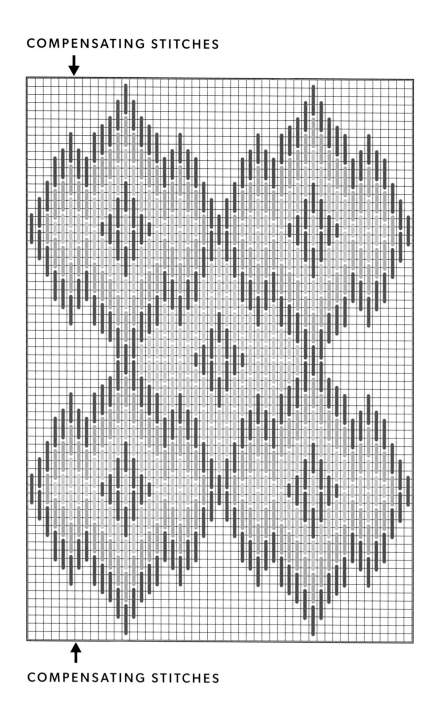

COMPENSATING STITCHES

KEY

White #Blanc

Dark turquoise #7596

Light turquoise #7598

REPEAT HORIZONTALLY × 4
REPEAT VERTICALLY × 2

BEGIN HERE

CENTRE

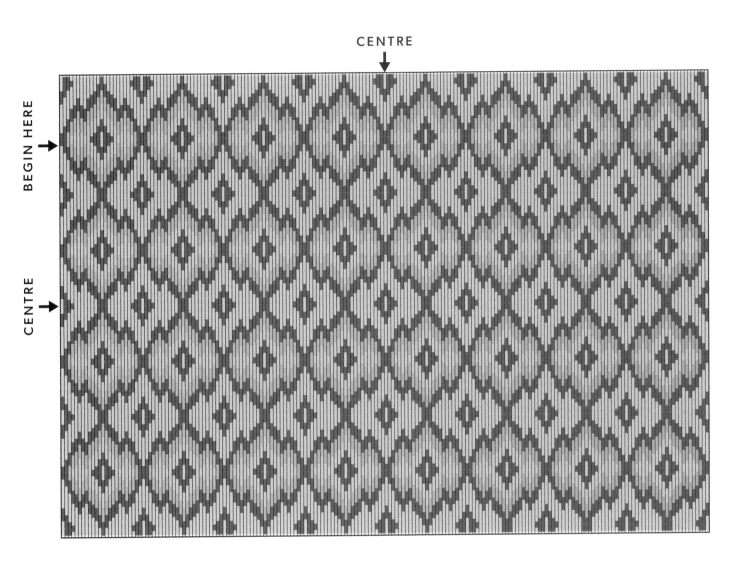

Zigzag Coin Purse

Purchasing a pre-finished purse makes creating a gift so easy. The simple wave stitching can work in many different colour combinations, from neon brights to soft pastels.

YOU'LL NEED

FABRIC

- Pre-finished stitch and zip coin purse (see Resources, page 138)

THREADS

- Pearl cotton #3
  (shown in DMC pearl cotton #3)
  One skein of each
      Dark grey #3799
      Medium blue grey #932
      White #Blanc
- Sewing thread

HABERDASHERY

- Tapestry needle #22
- Sewing needle
- Scissors

STITCHES USED

(pages 14–16)
- Zigzag Gobelin stitch
- Compensating stitches
- Tacking (basting) stitch

PREPARATION

(pages 17–18)
- Read the instructions from the manufacturer before beginning stitching
- Tack (baste) the vertical centre of the coin purse

FINISHED SIZE

4½ × 3in (11.5 × 7.5cm)

METHOD

Begin stitching using the dark grey pearl cotton at the centre stitch, 15 canvas threads below the top. Work the first zigzag row in dark grey, following the chart and colour key, working out to each side. This is the foundation row. Each stitch is worked side by side over 4 canvas threads in steps, each stepping up or down over 2 threads. Each subsequent row is worked the same way in the colours indicated, starting from either side.

Work compensating stitches at the top and bottom of the piece to fill in the canvas for a straight edge.

FINISHING

Follow the finishing instructions from the manufacturer.

ZIGZAG COIN PURSE CHART

CENTRE/BEGIN HERE 15 ROWS DOWN

CENTRE

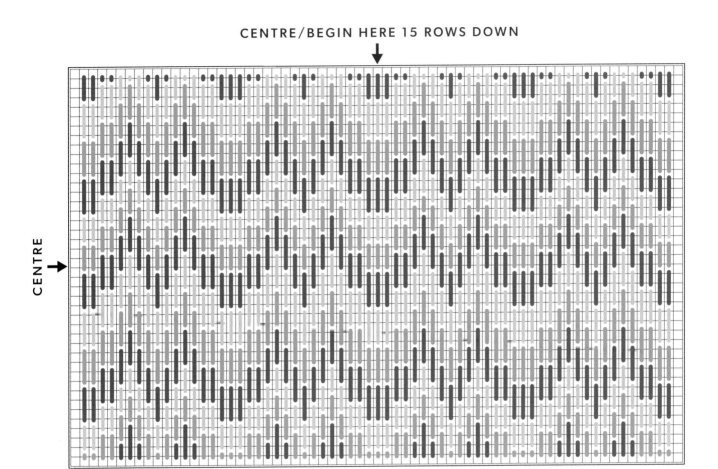

KEY

■ Dark grey #3799

■ Medium blue grey #932

□ White #Blanc

Heart Christmas Decoration

SKILL LEVEL – INTERMEDIATE

Working with embroidery floss on even-weave linen allows for more delicate stitching to create smaller projects. This petite ornament is finished with small pearl beads, a tassel and hanger.

YOU'LL NEED

FABRIC
- Two 8 × 9in (20 × 23cm) pieces 18-count white even-weave linen

THREADS
- Six-strand embroidery thread (shown in DMC stranded cotton)
  Two skeins
  - Red #666
  One skein of each
  - Dark green #905
  - Light green #166
  - White #Blanc
- Pearl cotton #8 (shown in DMC pearl cotton #8)
  One skein
  - White #Blanc
- Sewing thread

HABERDASHERY
- Tapestry needle #22
- Sewing needle or sewing machine
- Scissors
- Small amount of fibrefill for stuffing
- About eighty $\frac{1}{8}$in (3mm) diameter pearl seed beads
- 9in (23cm) white rat tail cord

STITCHES USED
(pages 14–16)
- Zigzag Gobelin stitch
- Tacking (basting) stitch
- Backstitch

PREPARATION
(pages 17–18)
- Tack (baste) to mark the centre of one piece of fabric

FINISHED SIZE
4in (10cm) square

METHOD

Using 6 strands of embroidery thread, each stitch is worked over the fabric by referring to the chart. Start stitching at the centre. Each stitch is worked over 4 fabric threads side by side. Follow the chart for the colour sequence.

FINISHING

Remove the tacking (basting) threads. Press lightly on the wrong side on a padded surface.

To create the outline, count 6 fabric threads away from the design on all 4 sides. Using pearl cotton, work a diagonal row of backstitches over 2 threads each, to form a diamond. Backstitch the same diamond dimensions on the unstitched piece of fabric. Trim the fabric to ½in (1.25cm) from the backstitch lines. Fold the fabric along the backstitch lines on both pieces. Press. With wrong sides together, line up the backstitches. Attach the pearl cotton on the wrong side of one piece, two stitches after the corner; slip the needle through the tops of the backstitches, threading a bead at the same time. Pull tightly so the bead is secure. Repeat for every stitch around 3 sides. Stuff with fibrefill. Sew the 4th side closed in the same manner to 4 stitches from the end. Fold the cord in half and insert into the opening at the corner. Sew the remaining backstitches, making sure to firmly catch the cord. Fasten securely.

TASSEL

Make a tassel from one end of the skein of embroidery thread.

1 Cut 2 × 12in (30cm) lengths of embroidery thread and thread one strand of cut embroidery thread through the loop at the top of the skein. Make a double knot to secure.

2 Take the second strand of cut thread and wrap around the top of the skein. Tie securely. Using a needle, hide the ends of this thread by pushing the needle into the wrap and pointing it downwards into the middle of the skein.

3 Slide the label down 3in (7.5cm) from the top. Cut above the label.

Sew the tassel to the decoration opposite the cord loop.

1   2   3

HEART CHRISTMAS DECORATION CHART

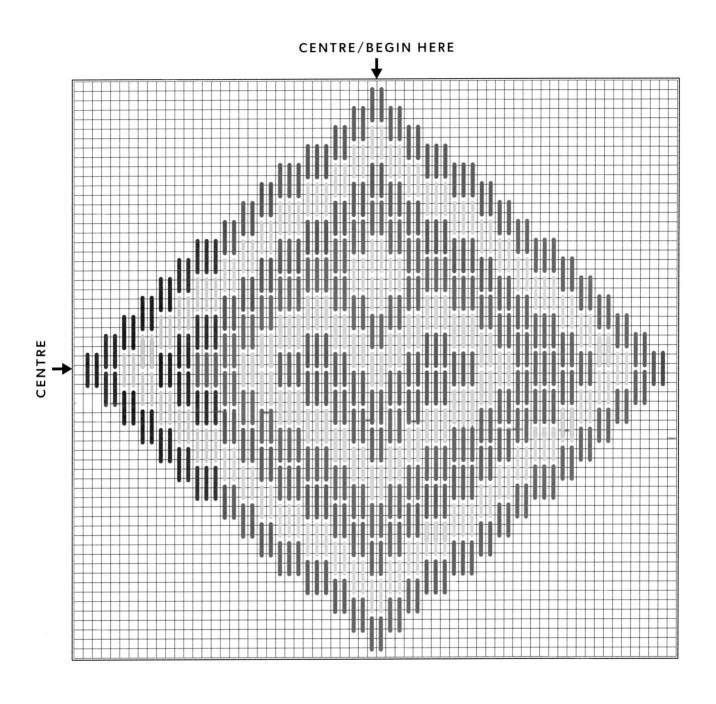

CENTRE/BEGIN HERE

CENTRE

KEY

■ Red #666

■ Dark green #905

□ Light green #166

□ White #Blanc

Jazzy Wave Key Fob

SKILL LEVEL – INTERMEDIATE

Riffing on traditional flame stitch, this colourful diamond begins as a square. The corners are folded, envelope style, to the back and sewn together. Filled with pot pourri, it also makes a perfect sachet.

YOU'LL NEED

FABRIC
- One 8 x 8in (20 x 20cm) piece 18-count white even-weave linen

THREADS
- Pearl cotton #3
  (shown in DMC pearl cotton #3)
  One skein of each
  - Dark pink #3687
  - Medium pink #899
  - Light pink #3689
  - Teal #924
  - Green #502
  - Blue #800
  - Dark gold #729
  - Medium gold #834
  - Yellow #745
- Six-strand embroidery thread
  (shown in DMC stranded cotton)
  One skein
  - Yellow #745
- Sewing thread

HABERDASHERY
- Masking tape
- Small amount of fibrefill for stuffing
- Tapestry needle #22
- Sewing needle or sewing machine
- Scissors
- 9in (23cm) pink rat tail cord

STITCHES USED
(pages 14–16)
- Zigzag Gobelin stitch
- Compensating stitches
- Tacking (basting) stitch
- Overcast stitch
- Slip stitch

PREPARATION
(pages 17–18)
- Tape the edges of the canvas using masking tape
- Tack (baste) a line 71 threads wide × 72 threads high (about 4in [10cm] square) to mark the stitching area

FINISHED SIZE
3in (7.5cm) square

METHOD

Using 1 strand of green pearl cotton #3, each stitch is worked over the canvas by referring to the chart. Start at the stitches indicated by the arrow, 4 threads down from the tacking (basting) line on the side. Each stitch is worked over 4 canvas threads side by side. Follow the chart for the colour sequence.

Work compensating stitches at the top and bottom of the piece to fill in for a straight edge.

FINISHING

Remove the tacking (basting) threads. Press lightly on the wrong side on a padded surface. Trim the canvas to ½in (1.25cm) from the stitching. Fold the raw canvas to the wrong side on all 4 sides, mitring the corners. Tack in place. With the wrong side facing, fold all 4 corners to meet in the centre.

Fold the cord in half and sew to the top corner. Using 2 strands of embroidery thread and overcast stitch, sew the edges together from the centre out to the corners, leaving half the seam open on the final seam. Insert the stuffing, then hand sew the opening closed with slip stitches.

JAZZY WAVE KEY FOB CHART

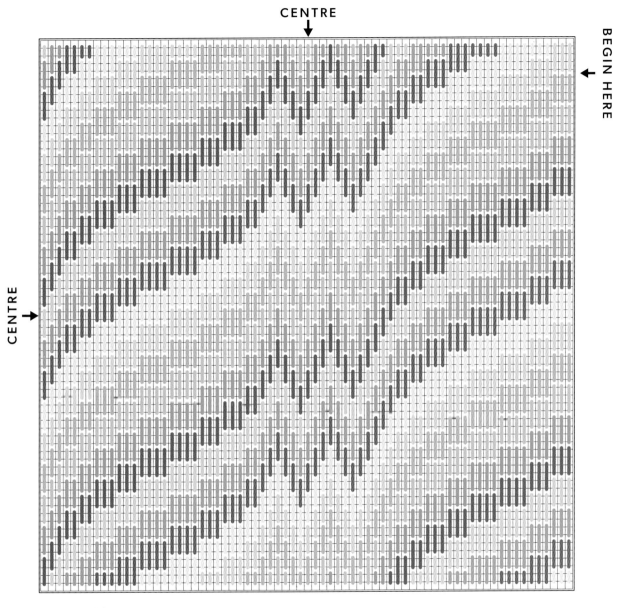

KEY

- ▨ Dark pink #3687
- ▨ Medium pink #899
- ▨ Light pink #3689
- ▨ Teal #924
- ▨ Green 502
- ▨ Blue #800
- ▨ Dark gold #729
- ▨ Medium gold #834
- ▨ Yellow #745

Zigzag Cosmetic Purse

SKILL LEVEL – EASY

Spring shades of peach, pink, mint and moss combine to create a striking pattern that's stitched onto a pre-finished purse, making this an easy project to complete.

YOU'LL NEED

FABRIC

- Pre-finished stitch and zip purse (see Resources, page 138)

THREADS

- Pearl cotton #3
  (shown in DMC pearl cotton #3)
  One skein of each
  - Dark green #3347
  - Pink #225
  - Dark pink #760
  - Light green #772
- Sewing thread

HABERDASHERY

- Tapestry needle #22
- Sewing needle
- Scissors

STITCHES USED

(pages 14–16)
- Zigzag Gobelin stitch
- Compensating stitches
- Tacking (basting) stitch

PREPARATION

(pages 17–18)
- Read the instructions from the manufacturer before beginning stitching
- Tack (baste) the vertical centre of the coin purse

FINISHED SIZE

6¾ × 4½in (17 × 11.5cm)

METHOD

Start at the stitches indicated by the arrow, 4 threads down from the tacking (basting) line on the side. Work the first row in dark green following the chart and colour key, working to the other side. This is the foundation row. Each stitch is worked side by side over 4 canvas threads in steps. Each subsequent row is worked the same way in the colours indicated, working from either side.

Work compensating stitches at the top and bottom of the piece to fill in for a straight edge.

FINISHING

Remove the tacking (basting) stitches. Follow the finishing instructions from the manufacturer.

ZIGZAG COSMETIC PURSE CHART

Please note split charts overlap in the centre

CENTRE

BEGIN HERE

CENTRE

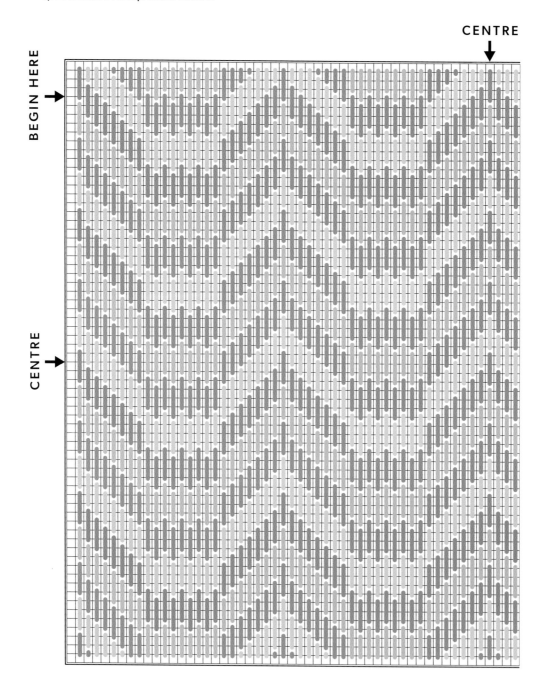

KEY

Dark green #3347

Pink #225

Dark pink #760

Light green #772

Mitred Christmas Ornament

SKILL LEVEL – EASY

**Repeating a simple motif in all four directions creates
a pretty Christmas star. Tiny pearl beads finish the edges and
are easy to sew on during finishing.**

YOU'LL NEED

FABRIC
- Two 8 × 9in (20 × 23cm) pieces 18-count white even-weave linen

THREADS
- Six-strand embroidery thread
  (shown in DMC stranded cotton)
  Two skeins
    Red #666
  One skein of each
    Dark green #905
    Light green #166
    White #Blanc
- Pearl cotton #8
  (shown in DMC pearl cotton #8)
  One skein
    White #Blanc
- Sewing thread

HABERDASHERY
- Tapestry needle #22
- Sewing needle
- Scissors
- Small amount of fibrefill for stuffing
- About 80 pearl seed beads, ⅛in (3mm) in diameter
- 9in (23cm) white rat tail cord

STITCHES USED
(pages 14–16)
- Zigzag Gobelin stitch
- Tacking (basting) stitch
- Backstitch

PREPARATION
(pages 17–18)
- Tack (baste) a square to mark a stitching area allowing for 68 threads to be worked over in each direction
- Tack to mark the centre
- Tack diagonal lines, working each tacking stitch over and under 2 diagonal threads

FINISHED SIZE
3¼in (8cm) square

METHOD

Using 6 strands of embroidery thread, each stitch is worked over the fabric by referring to the chart. Each stitch is worked over 4 fabric threads side by side. Please note that the design is worked on only one piece of fabric. Follow the chart for the colour sequence. Begin at the top centre, 3 stitches down from the tacking (basting) line, and work the red outline. Turn the fabric and work the red outline for the second quadrant, working vertically. Repeat the red outline for the remaining 2 quadrants. Fill in the remaining stitches, following the chart.

FINISHING

Remove the tacking (basting) threads. Press lightly on the wrong side on a padded surface.

Sew the pearl to the centre of the stitching. To create the outline, count 2 fabric threads away from the design on all 4 sides. Using pearl cotton, work a diagonal row of backstitches over 2 threads each, to form a diamond. Backstitch the same diamond dimensions on the unstitched piece of fabric. Trim fabric to ½in (1.25cm) from the backstitch lines. Fold the fabric along the backstitch lines on both pieces. Press. With wrong sides together, line up the backstitches. Attach the pearl cotton on the wrong side of one piece, two stitches after the corner; slip the needle through tops of the backstitches, threading a bead at the same time. Pull tightly so the bead is secure. Repeat for every stitch around 3 sides. Stuff with fibrefill. Sew the 4th side closed in the same manner to 4 stitches from the end. Fold the cord in half and insert into the opening at the corner. Sew the remaining backstitches, making sure to firmly catch the cord. Fasten securely.

TASSEL

Make a tassel from one end of the skein of embroidery thread.

1 Cut 2 × 12in (30cm) lengths of embroidery thread and thread one strand of cut embroidery thread through the loop at the top of the skein. Make a double knot to secure.

2 Take the second strand of cut thread and wrap around the top of the skein. Tie securely. Using a needle, hide the ends of this thread by pushing the needle into the wrap and pointing it downwards into the middle of the skein.

3 Slide the label down 3in (7.5cm) from the top. Cut above the label.

Sew the tassel to the ornament, opposite the cord loop.

MITRED CHRISTMAS ORNAMENT CHART

CENTRE/BEGIN HERE

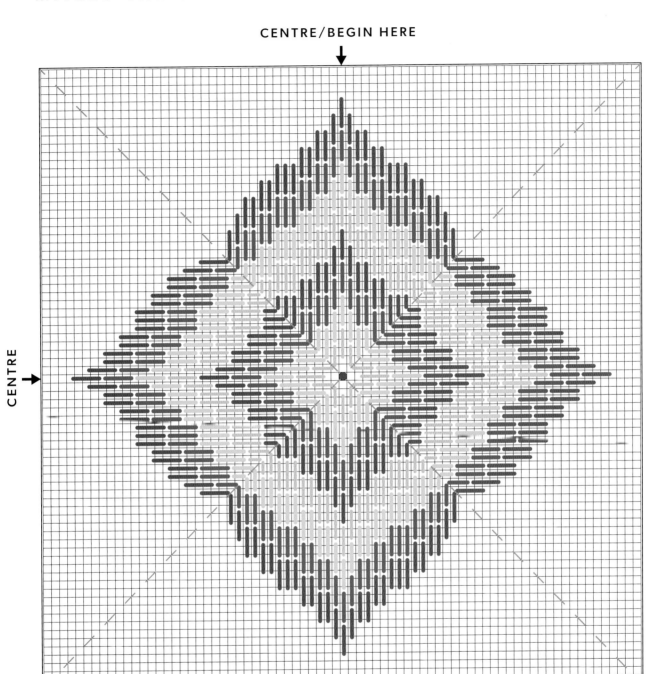

CENTRE

KEY

- ■ Red #666
- ■ Dark green #905
- ▨ Light green #166
- ▨ White #Blanc
- – – Tacking (basting) lines

Blue Wave Glasses Case

SKILL LEVEL – EASY

Using a pre-finished glasses case and filling it in with Bargello is fast and easy. This one makes a useful case to use yourself or give as a practical gift. Use cotton thread or tapestry wool for the best coverage.

YOU'LL NEED

FABRIC

- Pre-finished stitch and zip glasses case (see Resources, page 138)

THREADS

- Matt cotton
  (shown in DMC Retors mat cotton)
  One skein of each
  Very dark blue #2824
  Dark blue #2826
  Medium blue #2799
  Light blue #2828
  White #Blanc
- Sewing thread

HABERDASHERY

- Tapestry needle #22
- Sewing needle
- Scissors

STITCHES USED

(pages 14–16)
- Zigzag Gobelin stitch
- Compensating stitches
- Tacking (basting) stitch
- Overcast stitch

PREPARATION

(pages 17–18)
- Read the instructions from the manufacturer before beginning stitching
- Tack (baste) the vertical centre of the glasses case

FINISHED SIZE

3½ × 7in (9 × 18cm)

METHOD

Begin stitching using the matt cotton at the arrow on the left side, 10 canvas threads below the top. Work the first zigzag row in very dark blue, following the chart and colour key. This is the foundation row. Each stitch is worked over 4 canvas threads in steps, each stepping up or down over 2 threads. The stitches are worked in blocks of 3, 2, or 1 stitches, each lying side by side. Each subsequent row is worked in exactly the same way in the colours indicated.

Work compensating stitches at the top and bottom of the piece to fill in for a straight edge. Ignore the row marked "overcast stitches" on the chart at this stage.

FINISHING

Work a row of overcast stitches in white at the top through a double thickness of canvas. Follow the finishing instructions from the manufacturer.

BLUE WAVE GLASSES CASE CHART

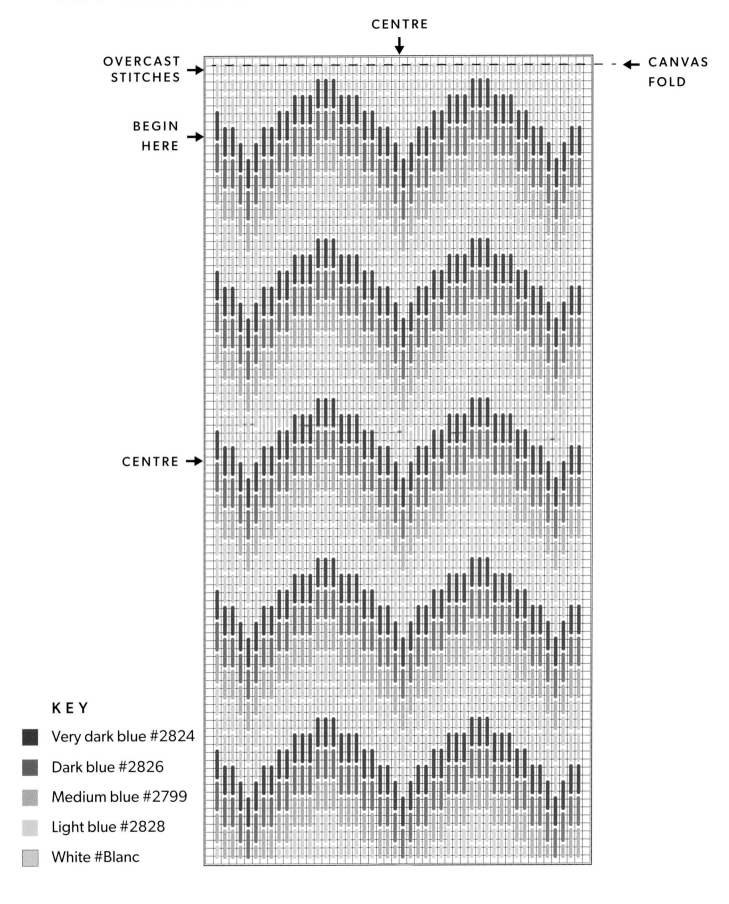

CENTRE

OVERCAST STITCHES

CANVAS FOLD

BEGIN HERE

CENTRE

KEY

- Very dark blue #2824
- Dark blue #2826
- Medium blue #2799
- Light blue #2828
- White #Blanc

Handy Needle Case

SKILL LEVEL – INTERMEDIATE

For centuries, embroiderers have protected their precious needles in handmade cases. A version of classic flame stitch makes a striking cover, with a layer of felt inside to hold the needles and a ribbon tie.

YOU'LL NEED

FABRIC
- 11 × 8in (28 × 20cm) piece 18-count white mono canvas
- 11 × 8in (28 × 20cm) piece orange fabric for lining
- 3 × 6in (7.5 × 15cm) piece white felt for leaves

THREADS
- Matt cotton
  (shown in DMC Retors mat cotton)
  One skein of each
  Terracotta #2360
  Medium orange #2351
  Light orange #2741
  Dark yellow #2742
  Medium yellow #2743
  Light yellow #2745
- Sewing thread

HABERDASHERY
- Masking tape
- Tapestry needle #22
- Sewing needle or sewing machine
- Scissors and pinking shears
- 24in (61cm) of ¼in (6mm) wide orange satin ribbon

STITCHES USED
(pages 14–16)
- Zigzag Gobelin stitch
- Compensating stitches
- Tacking (basting) stitch
- Backstitch
- Slip stitch

PREPARATION
(pages 17–18)
- Tape the edges of the canvas using masking tape
- Tack (baste) a line 125 threads wide × 76 threads high (about 7 × 4in [18 × 10cm]) to mark the stitching area
- Tack to mark the centre

FINISHED SIZE
3½ × 4in (9 × 10cm) folded

METHOD

Using 1 strand of terracotta mat cotton, each stitch is worked over the canvas by referring to the chart. Start at the stitches indicated by the arrow. Each stitch is worked over 4 canvas threads side by side, stepping up or down 2 fabric threads. Follow the chart for the colour sequence.

Work compensating stitches at the top and bottom of the piece to fill in for a straight edge.

FINISHING

Remove the tacking (basting) threads. Press lightly on the wrong side on a padded surface. Trim the canvas to ½in (1.25cm) from the stitching line. Place the right side of the backing fabric and the right side of the stitched piece together.

Tack around all sides. Machine stitch or use tiny backstitches to sew around 3 sides and ½in (1.25cm) in from each side on the bottom side. Remove the tacking thread and trim the backing fabric to the same size as the canvas. Trim across the corners. Turn to the right side, square out the corners; then hand sew the opening closed with slip stitches.

Trim the edges of the felt with pinking shears. Centre the felt on the inside of the lining. Tack in place. Using small running stitches, sew down the centre line to attach the felt to the needle case. Cut the ribbon in half. Following the photograph, make 2 folds at one end of the ribbon; tack in place. Sew the folded end of the ribbon to the centre of the front. Repeat for the back. Tie into a bow.

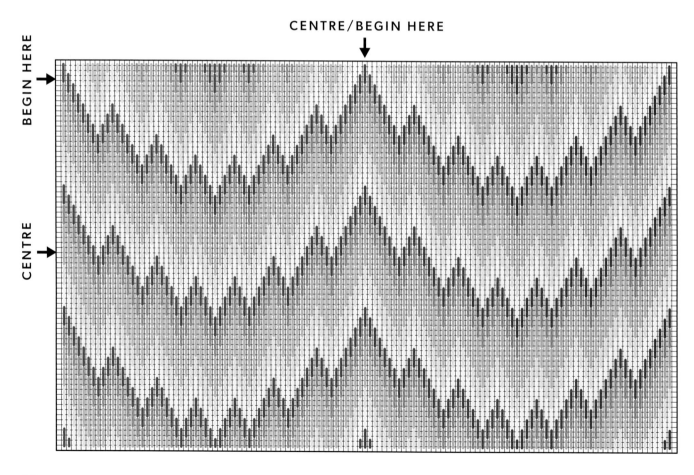

HANDY NEEDLE CASE CHART

COMPENSATING STITCHES

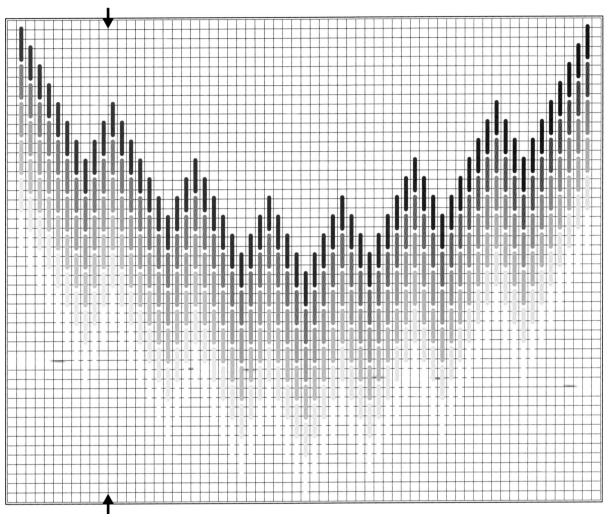

COMPENSATING STITCHES

REPEAT HORIZONTALLY × 2
REPEAT VERTICALLY × 2

KEY

Terracotta #2360

Medium orange #2351

Light orange #2741

Dark yellow #2742

Medium yellow #2743

Light yellow #2745

Vibrant Plant Holder

SKILL LEVEL – EASY

Plastic canvas makes a sturdy base for this striking cylindrical plant pot cover. The canvas is easy to work with, and the edges are quickly finished with overcast stitch.

YOU'LL NEED

FABRIC
- $10\frac{5}{8} \times 13\frac{5}{8}$ in (27 × 34.6cm) sheet 10-count clear plastic canvas

THREADS
- Persian wool
  (shown in Paternayan Persian wool)
  Three skeins of each
    - Burgundy #920
    - Red #841
    - Dark orange #831
    - Light orange #813

HABERDASHERY
- Tapestry needle #18
- Sewing thread
- Scissors
- Pencil

STITCHES USED
(pages 14–16)
- Zigzag Gobelin stitch
- Gobelin stitch
- Compensating stitches
- Overcast stitch

PREPARATION
(pages 17–18)
- Place the canvas with the longer sides at the top and bottom. With a pencil, mark the vertical centre of the sheet

FINISHED SIZE
$4\frac{1}{4} \times 13\frac{5}{8}$ in (11 × 34.6cm)

METHOD

Using 2 strands of wool, each stitch is worked over the canvas by referring to the chart. Following the chart, work the dark burgundy stitches first to mark outlines of the circles. Each stitch is worked over 4 canvas threads side by side, stepping up or down 2 fabric threads. Follow the chart for the colour sequence.

Work compensating stitches at the top and bottom of the piece to fill in for a straight edge. Ignore the row marked "overcast stitches" on the chart at this stage.

FINISHING

Trim the canvas so there are 3 empty holes at the top edge and 2 empty holes at the bottom edge. Be sure to trim close to the bars. Overcast along both edges with 2 strands of light orange. Form the canvas into a cylinder, overlapping the 2 holes of the 2 side edges. Tack (baste). Using 2 strands of wool, work Gobelin stitches over the empty squares, sharing the holes of the last stitches worked on both sides. Slip over a container.

VIBRANT PLANT HOLDER CHART

Please note split charts overlap in the centre

OVERCAST STITCHES

CENTRE

CENTRE | **BEGIN HERE**

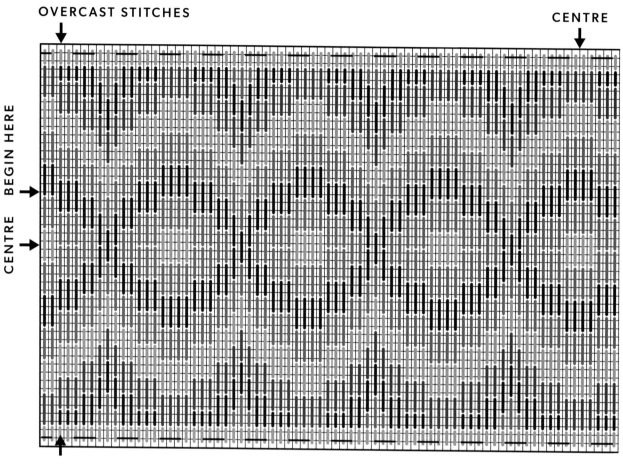

OVERCAST STITCHES

KEY

- ■ Burgundy #920
- ■ Red #841
- ▨ Dark orange #831
- ▨ Light orange #813

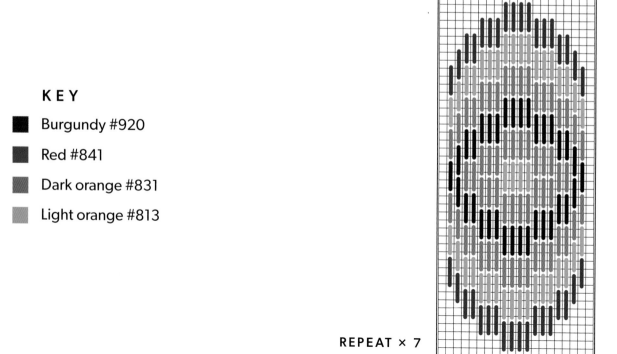

REPEAT × 7

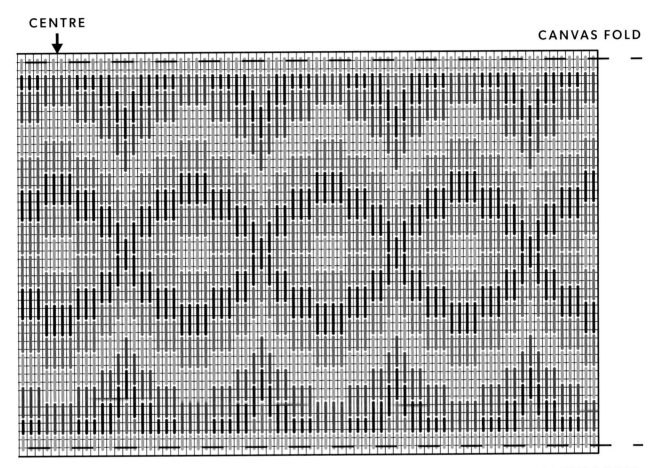

Mobile Phone Case

SKILL LEVEL – EASY

Moving Bargello stitches up and down makes it easy to create gentle curves. This pattern is inspired by an antique bell pull but using bright contrasting colours instead of the brown to take it to a new level.

YOU'LL NEED

FABRIC

- Two 7½ × 10in (19 × 25cm) pieces 18-count white mono canvas
- A4 (US Letter) sheet green adhesive felt

THREADS

- Pearl cotton #5
  (shown in DMC pearl cotton #5)
  One skein of each
  Dark green #700
  Medium green #703
  Light green #369
  Dark pink #602
  Light pink #604
- Sewing thread

HABERDASHERY

- Masking tape
- Tapestry needle #22
- Sewing needle or sewing machine
- Scissors

STITCHES USED

(pages 14–16)
- Zigzag Gobelin stitch
- Compensating stitches
- Tacking (basting) stitch
- Backstitch
- Overcast stitch

PREPARATION

(pages 17–18)
- Tape the edges of the canvas using masking tape
- Tack (baste) a line to mark 103 threads wide × 64 threads high (about 6 × 3½in [15 × 9cm]) to mark the stitching area on each piece

FINISHED SIZE

3½ × 6in (9 × 15cm)

METHOD

Using 2 strands of dark green cotton, each stitch is worked over the canvas by referring to the chart. Start at the stitches indicated by the arrow 18 threads down from the tacking line. Each stitch is worked over 4 canvas threads, side by side, stepping up or down 2 fabric threads. Work all the dark green stitches first, then fill in the remaining colours following the chart for the colour sequence.

Repeat as above on the second piece of canvas.

Work compensating stitches at the top and bottom of the pieces to fill in for a straight edge.

With dark green, work a row of backstitches over 2 threads down each side and across the bottom. Fold the upper edge of the canvas to the wrong side, leaving 3 rows of empty canvas threads at the top. Work a row of overcast stitches using dark green through both layers.

FINISHING

Press lightly on the wrong side on a padded surface. Trim canvas to ½in (1.25cm) round all sides. Fold the remaining sides to the wrong side and tack in place. Cut 2 pieces of felt, 5¼ × 3¼in (15.5 × 8cm) and glue to the wrong side of each piece. Remove the tacking threads.

With the wrong sides of both pieces of canvas facing, line up the backstitches. Attach the dark green thread to the wrong side of one piece, slip the needle through the tops of the backstitches and pull tightly. Continue around all 3 sides to close.

MOBILE PHONE CASE CHART

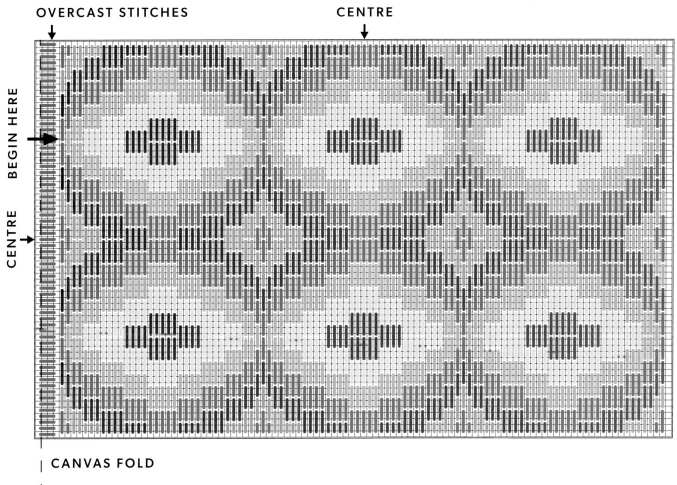

OVERCAST STITCHES   CENTRE

BEGIN HERE

CENTRE

CANVAS FOLD

KEY

- Dark green #700
- Medium green #703
- Light green #369
- Dark pink #602
- Light pink #604

Purple Pin Cushion

SKILL LEVEL – EASY

A tiny pillow makes a perfect pincushion for holding your sewing pins. Quick to stitch, this makes a great beginner project for new makers.

YOU'LL NEED

FABRIC
- 5in (13cm) square 18-count white mono canvas
- 5in (13cm) square purple cotton fabric for backing

THREADS
- Matt cotton
  (shown in DMC Retors mat cotton)
  One skein of each
    Dark purple #2531
    Medium purple #2532
    Light purple #2396
- Sewing thread

HABERDASHERY
- Masking tape
- Tapestry needle #22
- Sewing needle or sewing machine
- Small amount of fibrefill for stuffing
- Scissors

STITCHES USED
(pages 14–16)
- Zigzag Gobelin stitch
- Compensating stitches
- Tacking (basting) stitch
- Backstitch
- Slip stitch

PREPARATION
(pages 17–18)
- Tape the edges of the canvas using masking tape
- Tack (baste) a line 56 threads wide × 56 threads high (about 3in [7.5cm] square) to mark the stitching area
- Tack to mark the centre

FINISHED SIZE
3in (7.5cm) square

METHOD

Using 1 strand of mat cotton, each stitch is worked over the canvas by referring to the chart. Start at the stitches indicated by the arrow 12 stitches down from the tacking stitch on the left side. Each stitch is worked over 4 canvas threads side by side, stepping up or down 2 fabric threads. Follow the chart for the colour sequence.

Work compensating stitches at the top and bottom of the piece to fill in for a straight edge.

FINISHING

Remove the tacking threads. Press lightly on the wrong side on a padded surface. Trim the canvas to ½in (1.25cm) from the stitching.

Place the right side of the backing fabric and the right side of the stitched piece together. Tack around all sides. Machine stitch or use tiny backstitches to sew around 3 sides and ½in (1.25cm) in from each side on the 4th side. Remove the tacking thread and trim the backing fabric to the same size as the canvas. Trim across the corners. Turn to the right side, square out the corners; stuff and hand sew the opening closed with slip stitches.

PURPLE PIN CUSHION CHART

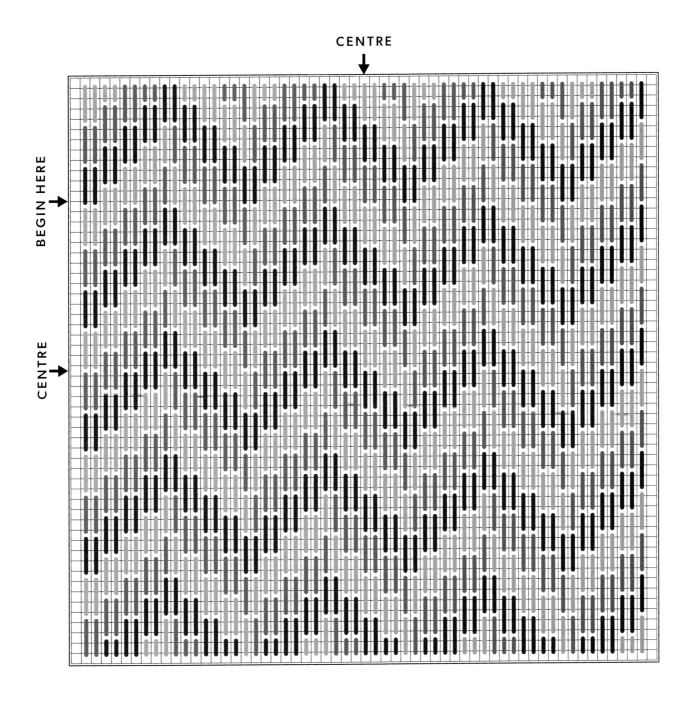

KEY

■ Dark purple #2531

■ Medium purple #2532

■ Light purple #2396

Rainbow Greeting Card

SKILL LEVEL – EASY

Purchased window cards are a great way to show off any Bargello patterns. Choose this bright rainbow, or make one of the other patterns in this book in the same size as this.

YOU'LL NEED

FABRIC

- 8in (20cm) square 18-count white mono canvas

THREADS

- Six-strand embroidery thread (shown in DMC stranded cotton)
  One skein of each
  - Red #606
  - Orange #970
  - Yellow #973
  - Green #703
  - Blue #995
  - Purple #208
  - Magenta #3804
- Sewing thread

HABERDASHERY

- Masking tape
- Tapestry needle #22
- Sewing needle
- Scissors
- Frame card 4¼ × 5½in (11 × 14cm) with opening 3 × 4¾in (7.5cm × 12.5cm)

STITCHES USED

(pages 14–16)
- Zigzag Gobelin stitch
- Compensating stitches
- Tacking (basting) stitch

PREPARATION

(pages 17–18)
- Tape the edges of the canvas using masking tape
- Tack (baste) a line 76 threads wide × 60 threads high (about 4¼ × 3¼in [11 × 8.5cm] square) to mark the stitching area

FINISHED SIZE

Stitching area 4¼ × 3¼in (11 × 8.5cm)

METHOD

Using 6 strands of embroidery thread, each stitch is worked over 4 canvas threads side by side, stepping up or down 2 fabric threads. Start at the stitches indicated by the arrow 4 stitches down from the tacking stitch on the left side. Follow the chart for the colour sequence.

Work compensating stitches at the top and bottom of the piece to fill in for a straight edge.

FINISHING

Remove the tacking threads. Press lightly on the wrong side on a padded surface. Trim the canvas to ½in (1.25cm) from the stitching. Slip the canvas into the card opening.

RAINBOW GREETING CARD CHART

CENTRE

BEGIN HERE

CENTRE

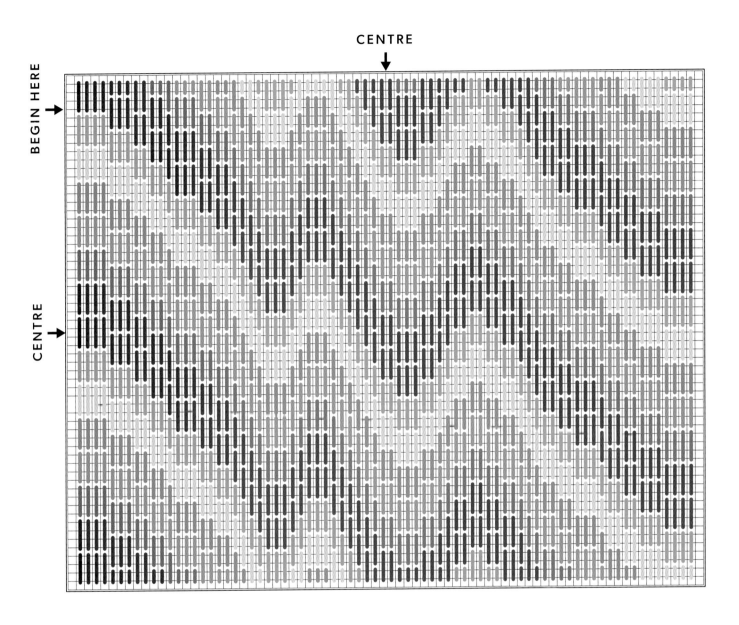

KEY

■ Red #606

■ Orange #970

■ Yellow #973

■ Green #703

■ Blue #995

■ Purple #208

■ Magenta #3804

Rainbow Wave Hoop

SKILL LEVEL – EASY

Embroidery hoops make a perfect frame for Bargello stitching.
They are easy to hang and make great gifts for family and friends.
Think about a colour combination that will suit the recipient.

YOU'LL NEED

FABRIC
- 10in (25cm) square 18-count white mono canvas
- 6in (15cm) diameter circle white felt for backing

THREADS
- Pearl cotton #3
  (shown in DMC pearl cotton #3}
  One skein of each
       Red #606
       Orange #970
       Yellow #743
       Green #987
       Blue #797
       Purple #3803
       White #Blanc
- Sewing thread
- White pearl cotton #5
  (shown in DMC pearl cotton) for finishing
   back of hoop

HABERDASHERY
- Masking tape
- 6in (15cm) embroidery hoop
- Tapestry needle #22
- Embroidery needle #6
- Sewing needle
- Scissors

STITCHES USED
(pages 14–16)
- Zigzag Gobelin stitch
- Tacking stitch

PREPARATION
(pages 17–18)
- Tape the edges of the canvas using masking tape
- Centre the canvas in the hoop, assembling it securely

FINISHED SIZE
6in (15cm) diameter

METHOD

Using 1 strand of pearl cotton #3 and the tapestry needle, each stitch is worked over the canvas by referring to the chart. Start at the red stitches indicated by the arrow at the right side of the chart. Each stitch is worked over 4 canvas threads forming blocks of stitches 4 threads tall side by side, in groups of 4, 3, 2 and 1, stepping down 2 fabric threads for each block. Follow the chart for the colour sequence.

FINISHING

Remove the tape. Trim the canvas to a circle, leaving at least 2in (5cm) of canvas beyond the stitching. With a long length of pearl cotton #5 and the wrong side facing, insert the embroidery needle into the canvas ½in (1.25cm) from the outer edge of the hoop. Secure with several double stitches and work a circle of running stitches around the perimeter of the hoop, leaving a long tail.

Trim off any excess canvas at least ½in (1.25cm) from the running stitches. Gather the running stitches by pulling the pearl cotton until the canvas fits snugly around the inner hoop. Secure the thread.

Place the felt backing on top of the canvas and, using red pearl cotton #606 and the embroidery needle, slip stitch through both felt and canvas layers to attach the backing.

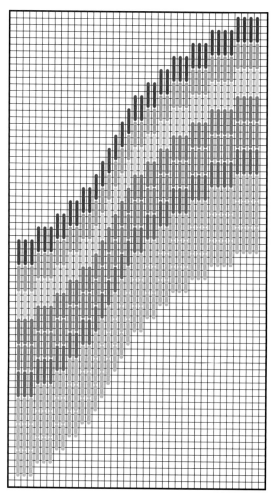

REPEAT UNTIL THE HOOP IS FILLED

RAINBOW WAVE HOOP CHART

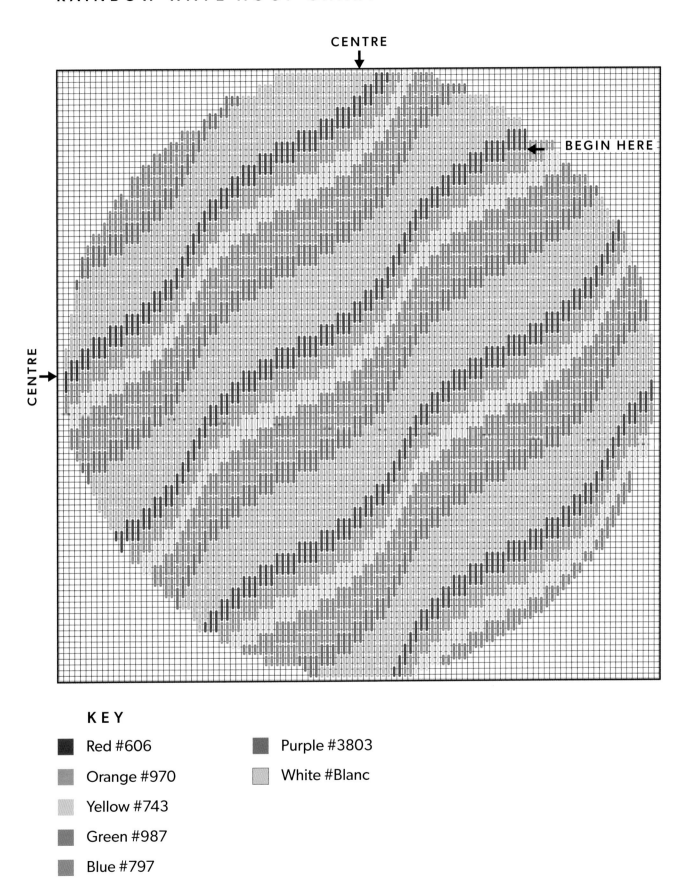

KEY

■ Red #606	■ Purple #3803
■ Orange #970	▨ White #Blanc
▨ Yellow #743	
■ Green #987	
■ Blue #797	

Red, White and Blue Pin Cushion

SKILL LEVEL – EASY

Pin cushions make wonderful gifts for creative friends.
Working a small stitch area is a great way to try out Bargello,
and then to turn it into something useful.

YOU'LL NEED

FABRIC

- 8in (20cm) square 18-count white mono canvas
- 8in (20cm) square cranberry velvet for backing

THREADS

- Matt cotton
  (shown in DMC Retors mat cotton)
  One skein of each
  Dark blue #2824
  Medium blue #2827
  Light blue #2800
  Light pink #2818
  Medium pink #2776
  Dark pink #2572
  Cranberry #2570
  White #Blanc
- Sewing thread

HABERDASHERY

- Masking tape
- Tapestry needle #22
- Sewing needle or sewing machine
- Scissors

- Small amount of fibrefill for stuffing
- 18in (46cm) white rat tail cord

STITCHES USED

(pags 14–16)
- Zigzag Gobelin stitch
- Compensating stitches
- Tacking (basting) stitch
- Backstitch
- Slip stitch

PREPARATION

(pages 17–18)
- Tape the edges of the canvas using masking tape
- Tack (baste) a line 73 threads wide × 71 threads high (about 4in [10cm] square) to mark the stitching area
- Tack to mark the centre

FINISHED SIZE

4in (10cm) square

METHOD

Using 1 strand of mat cotton, each stitch is worked over the canvas by referring to the chart. Start at the stitches indicated by the arrow or at the centre. Each stitch is worked over 4 canvas threads side by side, forming peaks and valleys. Follow the chart for the colour sequence.

Work compensating stitches at the top and bottom of the piece to fill in for a straight edge.

FINISHING

Remove the tacking threads. Press lightly on the wrong side on a padded surface. Trim the canvas to ½in (1.25cm) from the stitching.

Place the right side of the backing fabric and the right side of the stitched piece together. Tack round all sides. Machine stitch or use tiny backstitches to sew around 3 sides and ½in (1.25cm) in from each side on the 4th side. Remove the tacking thread and trim the backing. Trim across the corners. Turn to the right side, square out the corners; insert the stuffing and hand sew the opening closed with slip stitches.

With white sewing thread slip stitch the rat tail cord over the seam.

RED, WHITE AND BLUE PIN CUSHION CHART

CENTRE

BEGIN HERE

CENTRE

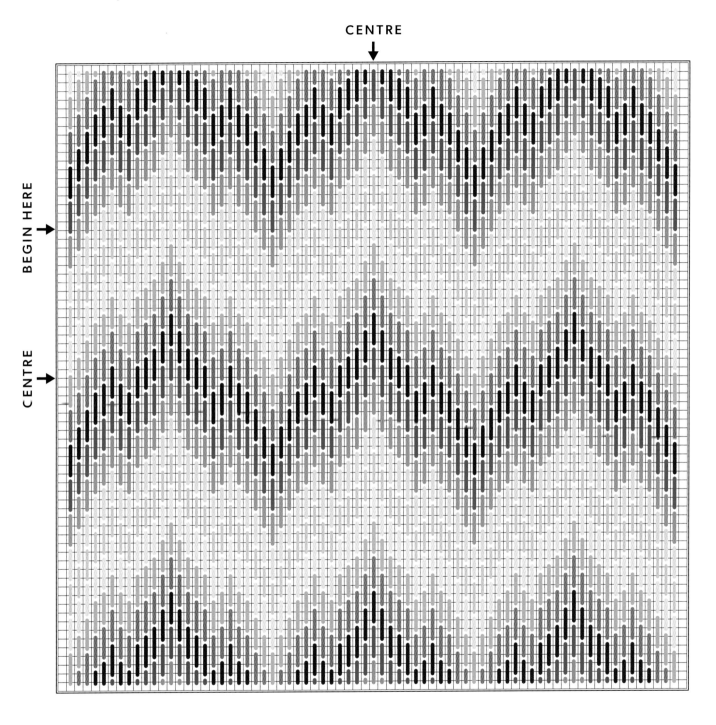

KEY

Dark blue #2824

Medium blue #2827

Light blue #2800

Light pink #2818

Medium pink #2776

Dark pink #2572

Cranberry #2570

White #Blanc

Ribbon Hand Towel

SKILL LEVEL – EASY

Worked vertically on the Aida band of a prefinished velour towel, this trompe-l'oeil design mimics a waving ribbon. You could do the embroidery on a piece of Aida, then sew it to a plain towel.

YOU'LL NEED

FABRIC

- Velour guest towel
(see Resources, page 130)

THREADS

- Pearl cotton #5
(shown in DMC pearl cotton #5)
One skein of each
    Dark blue #798
    Medium blue #334
    Light blue #827
    Pale blue #828
    White #Blanc
- Sewing thread

HABERDASHERY

- Tapestry needle #22
- Sewing needle or sewing machine
- Scissors

STITCHES USED

(pages 14–16)
- Zigzag Gobelin stitch
- Compensating stitches
- Tacking (basting) stitch

PREPARATION

(pages 17–18)
- Tack (baste) the Aida band to mark the centre

FINISHED SIZE

Towel is 12 × 19½in (30 × 49.5cm)

METHOD

Holding the Aida band vertically with the fringed side to the left, begin stitching 2 squares in from the upper left edge with dark blue thread, following the arrow on the chart. Each stitch is worked over 4 Aida squares, side by side, stepping down 2 Aida squares in groups of 1, 2, 3 and 4. Follow the chart for the colour sequence.

Work compensating stitches at the top and bottom of the piece to fill in for a straight edge.

FINISHING

Remove the tacking stitches. Lightly press the wrong side on a padded surface.

RIBBON HAND TOWEL CHART

Please note split charts overlap in the centre

- Dark blue #798
- Medium blue #334
- Light blue #827
- Pale blue #828
- White #Blanc

CENTRE

BEGIN HERE

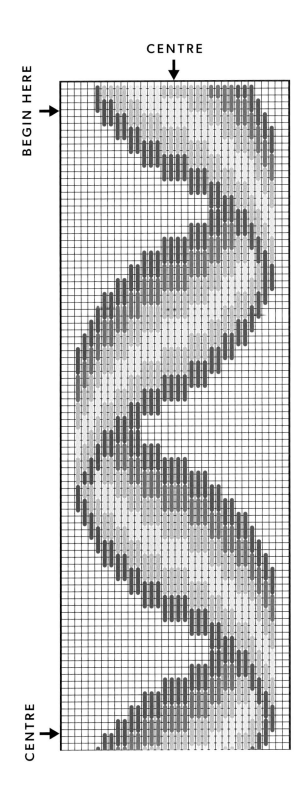

CENTRE

CENTRE

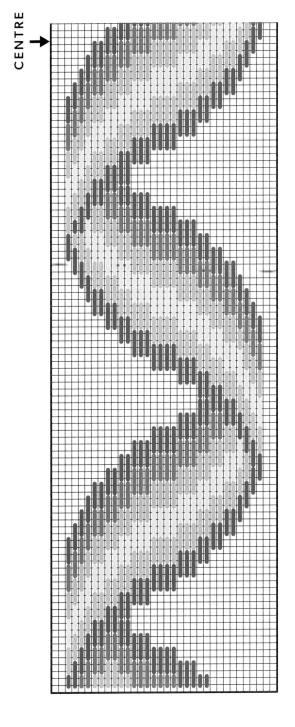

Traditional Scissors Case

SKILL LEVEL – INTERMEDIATE

A scissors case is functional as well as beautiful. The delicate blade points of embroidery scissors are easy to bend if not protected, and this small, lined case is perfect for safe keeping.

YOU'LL NEED

FABRIC
- 6 × 7in (15 × 18cm) piece 18-count white mono canvas
- 5½ × 4½in (14 × 11.5cm) piece green fabric for lining

THREADS
- Pearl cotton #3
  (shown in DMC pearl cotton #3)
  One skein of each
  - Yellow #745
  - Dark green #320
  - Light green #3348
  - Pale gold #613
  - Pink #3687
  - Peach #353
- Six-strand embroidery thread
  (shown in DMC stranded cotton)
  One skein
  - Dark green #523
- Sewing thread

HABERDASHERY
- Masking tape
- Tapestry needle #22
- Sewing thread and needle or sewing machine
- 20in (50cm) green satin ribbon, ¼in (6mm) wide
- Scissors

STITCHES USED
(pages 14–16)
- Zigzag Gobelin stitch
- Compensating stitches
- Tacking (basting) stitch
- Overcast stitch
- Backstitch

PREPARATION
(pages 17–18)
- Tape the edges of the canvas using masking tape
- Tack (baste) a line 94 threads wide × 70 threads high (about 5 x 4in [13 x 10cm]) to mark the stitching area
- Tack to mark the centre

FINISHED SIZE
2½ × 4in (6.5cm × 10cm) folded

METHOD

Using 1 strand of pale peach pearl cotton, each stitch is worked over the canvas by referring to the chart. Begin at the centre, working out to each side. Each stitch is worked over 4 canvas threads side by side. Follow the chart for the colour sequence.

Work compensating stitches at the top and bottom of the piece to fill in for a straight edge.

With 3 strands of embroidery thread, work a row of backstitches over 2 threads down each side and across the bottom. Fold the upper edge of the canvas to the wrong side, leaving 3 rows of empty canvas threads at the top. Work a row of overcast stitches using dark green pearl cotton through both layers.

FINISHING

Press lightly on the wrong side on a padded surface. Trim the canvas to ½in (1.25cm) from the stitching. Fold all the remaining edges to the wrong side and tack in place.

Lay the canvas with the wrong side facing. Fold the side edges to the centre back to form the case. Sew the back seam first, then the bottom seam. Line up the backstitches, and with 3 strands of embroidery floss, slip the needle through the top of the backstitches and pull tightly. Continue to sew the back seam, then ensure the seam is centred and sew the bottom edges closed with slip stitches. Remove the tacking threads.

Fold the lining fabric in half to match the shorter sides. With needle and thread or sewing machine and with a ¼in (6mm) seam sew along the side and bottom. Fold the top edge ¾in (19mm) to the wrong side. Press. Cut the ribbon in half and sew securely to the centre of each side. Slip the lining into the case and sew to the folded edge of the overcast stitches.

TRADITIONAL SCISSORS CASE CHART

CANVAS FOLD **CENTRE/BEGIN HERE** **OVERCAST STITCHES**

CENTRE

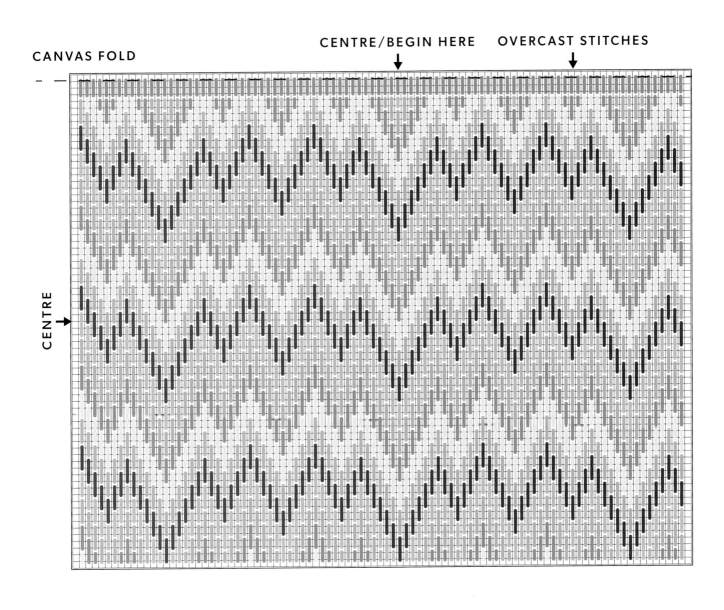

KEY

- Yellow #745
- Dark green #320
- Light green #3348
- Pale gold #613
- Pink #3687
- Peach #353

Stylish Shoulder Bag

SKILL LEVEL – INTERMEDIATE

Tile patterns were favoured by the aristocracy in the 1700s. This modern interpretation makes a stunning bag, perfect for holding a few small items for an evening out.

YOU'LL NEED

FABRIC

- 12 × 10in (30 × 25cm) piece 18-count white mono canvas
- 12 × 10in (30 × 25cm) piece burgundy velvet for backing
- 8½ × 13in (21.5 × 33cm) piece black silk for lining

THREADS

- Six-strand embroidery thread (shown in DMC stranded cotton)
  Two skeins
      Black #310
  One skein of each
      Dark terracotta #355
      Light terracotta #223
      Pale terracotta #224
      Pink #353
      Dark blue #931
      Light blue #3752
- Sewing thread

HABERDASHERY

- Masking tape
- Sewing needle or sewing machine
- Tapestry needle #22
- Scissors
- 42in (107cm) black parachute cord, ⅛in (3mm) diameter or decorative cord
- 4in (10cm) black rat tail cord
- Decorative black shank button, ½in (1.25cm) diameter
- 2 black tassels 2in (5cm) long

STITCHES USED

(pages 14–16)
- Zigzag Gobelin stitch
- Compensating stitches
- Tacking (basting) stitch

PREPARATION

(pages 17–18)
- Tape the edges of the canvas using masking tape
- Tack (baste) a line 151 threads wide × 116 threads high (about 8¼ × 6in [21cm × 15cm]) to mark the stitching area
- Tack to mark the centre

FINISHED SIZE

8¼ × 6in (21 × 15cm)

METHOD

Using 6 strands of thread, each stitch is worked over the canvas by referring to the chart. Start at the stitches indicated by the arrow or at the centre. Each stitch is worked over 4 canvas threads side by side, stepping up or down 2 fabric threads. Work all the black outlines first. Then fill in the remaining colours following the chart for the colour sequence.

Work compensating stitches at the top and bottom of the piece to fill in for a straight edge.

Fold the lining in half. Sew the side seams together with a ½in (1.25cm) seam. Fold the upper edge 1in (2.5cm) to the wrong side and press.

FINISHING

Fold the upper edge of the canvas to the wrong side, leaving 2 rows of empty canvas threads at the top. Using black, work a row of overcast stitches through both layers.

Remove the tacking threads. Press lightly on a padded surface. Trim the canvas to ½in (1.25cm) from the stitching. Place the right side of the backing fabric and the right side of the stitched piece together. Tack along the 2 sides and lower edge. Machine stitch or use tiny backstitches to sew around the 3 sides. Remove the tacking threads and trim the backing fabric to the same size as the canvas. Trim across the lower corners. Turn to the right side and square out the corners. Turn the top edge of the backing to the inside so both edges match.

Place the cord in each side of the bag, with 1in (2.5cm) to the inside. Sew in place. Using the photo as a guide, sew the button to the centre of the top. On the opposite side, sew the folded rat tail cord in place inside the bag, with the loop pointing upwards, to make a button loop.

Slip the lining into the bag and sew the folded edge to the bottom edge of the overcast stitches and to the backing. Attach the tassels securely to the top corners of the bag.

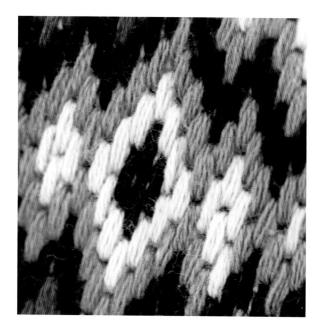

STYLISH SHOULDER BAG CHART

COMPENSATING STITCHES

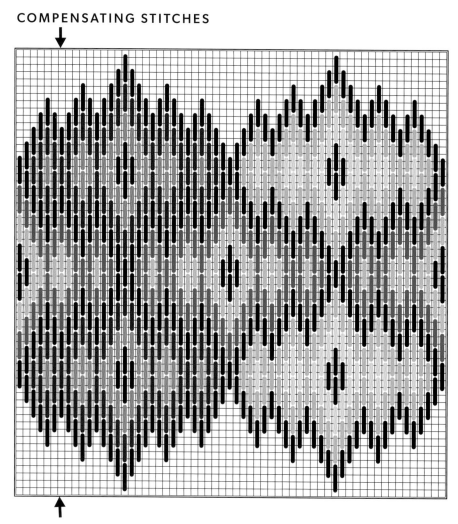

COMPENSATING STITCHES

REPEAT HORIZONTALLY × 2.5
REPEAT VERTICALLY × 2

KEY

- Black #310
- Dark terracotta #355
- Light terracotta #223
- Pale terracotta #224
- Pink #353
- Dark blue #931
- Light blue #3752

CENTRE

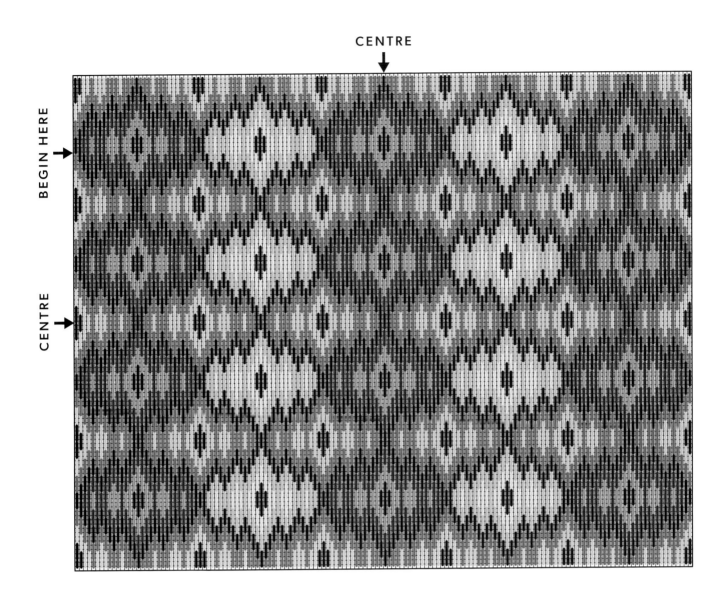

BEGIN HERE

CENTRE

Flower Vase Cover

SKILL LEVEL – EASY

Worked on plastic canvas, this vase cover fits over a cylindrical glass vase, which can have many uses. You could use it for knitting needles, paintbrushes or wooden spoons.

YOU'LL NEED

FABRIC

- 10⅝ × 13⅝ in (27 × 34.6cm) sheet 10-mesh clear plastic canvas

THREADS

- Persian wool
  (shown in Paternayan Persian wool)
  Three skeins of each
  - Dark turquoise #573
  - Light turquoise #578
  - Green #699
  - Yellow #760
- Sewing thread

HABERDASHERY

- Tapestry needle #18
- Sewing needle
- Scissors

STITCHES USED

(pages 14–16)
- Zigzag Gobelin stitch
- Compensating stitches
- Overcast stitch
- Slip stitch

PREPARATION

- Place the canvas with the longer sides at the top and bottom

FINISHED SIZE

6½ × 13⅝ in (16.5 × 34.6cm)

METHOD

Using 2 strands of wool, each stitch is worked over the canvas by referring to the chart. Working 2 holes in, begin with the dark turquoise stitches indicated by the arrow at the chart. This is the foundation row. Each stitch is worked over 4 canvas threads side by side, stepping up or down 2 fabric threads. Follow the chart for the colour sequence.

Work compensating stitches at the top and bottom of the piece to fill in for a straight edge. Ignore the row marked "overcast stitches" on the chart at this stage.

FINISHING

Trim the canvas so there are 3 empty holes at the top edge and 2 empty holes at the bottom edge. Be sure to trim close to the bars. Overcast along both edges with 2 strands of dark turquoise. Form the canvas into a cylinder, overlapping the two holes of the two side edges. Tack (baste). Using 2 strands of wool, work overcast stitches over the empty squares, sharing the holes of the last stitches worked on both sides. Slip over a container.

FLOWER VASE COVER CHART

Please note split charts overlap in the centre

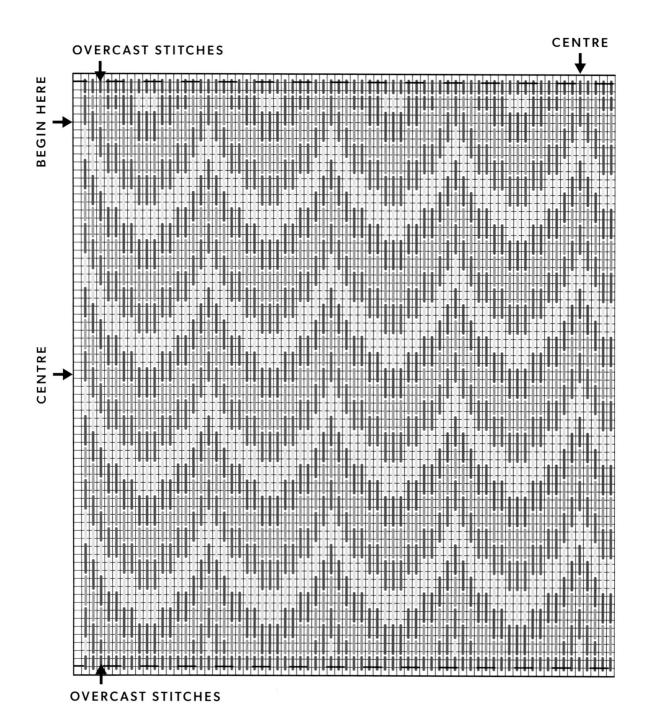

K E Y

Dark turquoise #573

Light turquoise #578

Green #699

Yellow #760

CENTRE

CANVAS FOLD

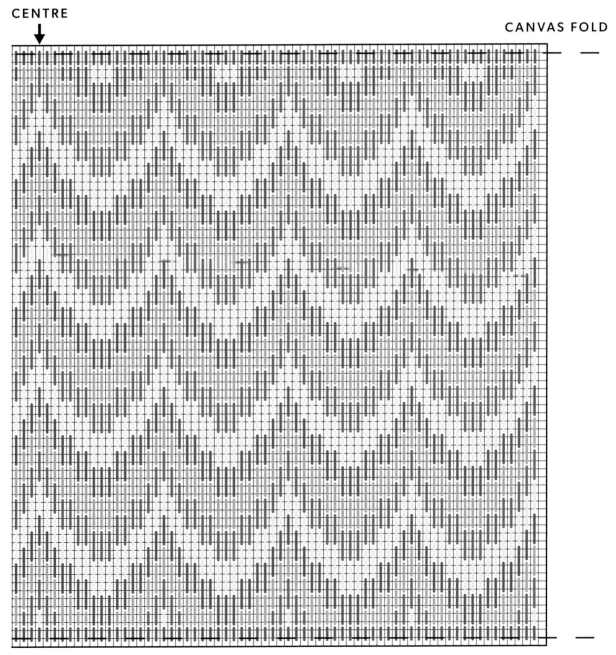

CANVAS FOLD

Southwestern Zigzag Pillow

SKILL LEVEL – EASY

I was inspired by the shades of the Southwest, but any three colours will work for this zigzag-patterned pillow, which makes a wonderful addition to any couch or occasional chair.

YOU'LL NEED

FABRIC

- 18in (46cm) square 14-count white mono canvas
- 18in (46cm) square cream velvet for backing

THREADS

- Tapestry wool
  (shown in DMC tapestry wool)
  Eight skeins of each
  - Turquoise #7956
  - Terracotta #7356
  - Light grey #7510
- Sewing thread

HABERDASHERY

- Masking tape
- Tapestry needle #20
- Sewing needle or sewing machine
- Scissors
- 15in (38cm) square pillow form

STITCHES USED

(pages 14–16)
- Zigzag Gobelin stitch
- Compensating stitches
- Tacking (basting) stitch
- Backstitch
- Slip stitch

PREPARATION

(pages 17–18)
- Tape the edges of the canvas using masking tape
- Tack (baste) a line to make a 14in (36cm) square to mark the stitching area

FINISHED SIZE

14in (36cm) square

METHOD

Using 1 strand of tapestry wool, each stitch is worked over the canvas by referring to the chart. Start at the turquoise stitches indicated by the arrow at the left side of the square, 8 threads down. This is the foundation row. Each stitch is worked over 4 canvas threads side by side, stepping up or down 2 fabric threads. Follow the chart for the colour sequence.

Work compensating stitches at the top and bottom of the piece to fill in for a straight edge.

FINISHING

Remove the tacking threads. Press lightly on the wrong side on a padded surface. Trim the canvas to ½in (1.25cm) from the stitching.

Place the right side of the backing fabric and the right side of the stitched piece together. Tack around all sides. Machine stitch or use tiny backstitches to sew around 3 sides and 1in (2.5cm) in from each side on the 4th side. Remove the tacking thread and trim the backing fabric to the same size as the canvas. Trim across the corners. Turn to the right side, square out the corners; insert the pillow form and hand sew the opening closed with slip stitches.

SOUTHWESTERN ZIGZAG PILLOW CHART

COMPENSATING STITCHES ON ALL SIDES

BEGIN HERE

REPEAT HORIZONTALLY × 3
REPEAT VERTICALLY × 15

CENTRE

CENTRE

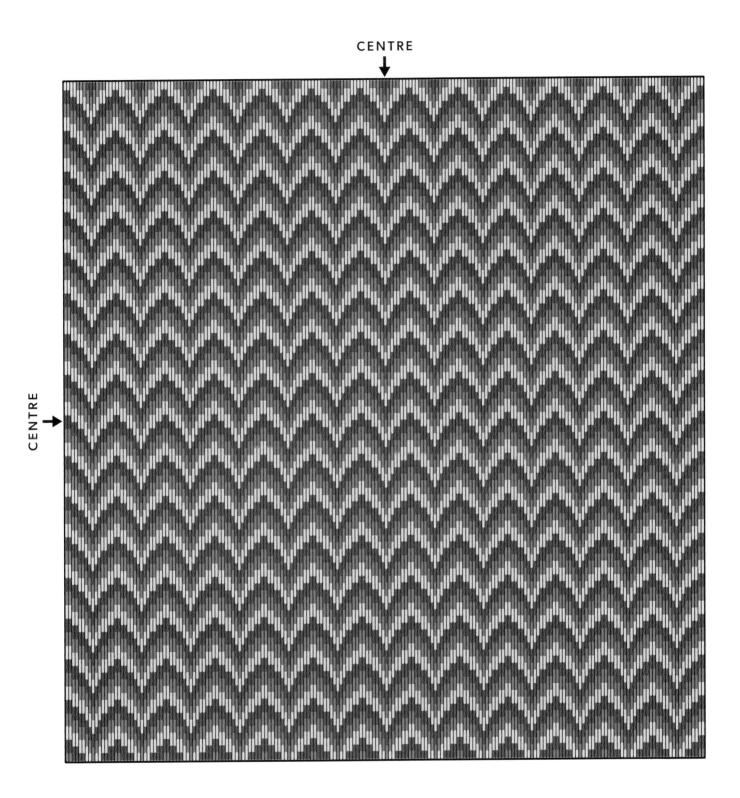

KEY

Turquoise #7956

Terracotta #7356

Light grey #7510

Resources

FABRIC, CANVAS, FELT, THREAD, TASSELS, CORDS AND EMBROIDERY HOOPS:
Amazon – amazon.co.uk / amazon.com
Hobbycraft – hobbycraft.co.uk

GREETINGS CARDS AND BEADS:
Amazon – amazon.co.uk / amazon.com
Dunelm – dunelm.com
Michaels – michaels.com

EMBROIDERY THREAD AND PEARL COTTON:
DMC – dmc.com

PRE-MADE STITCHING PIECES:
Stitch and Zip Kits – stitchandzipkits.com
Walmart – walmart.com
Amazon – amazon.co.uk / amazon.com
Alice Peterson – alicepetersoncompany.com

VELOUR TOWELS:
Charles Craft Maxton
Amazon – amazon.co.uk / amazon.com
DMC – dmc.com

Acknowledgements

I would like to thank the talented staff at Quail Publishing for creating such a beautiful book. Special thanks to my friend, Trisha Malcolm, for encouraging me to explore Bargello again, and thanks to my editors, Wendy Hobson and Sarah Perkins, and chart designer Joanne Aston and Jennifer Stephens for contributing to the artwork and the layout of the book. I could not have created these Bargello projects without the support of my family and friends who spurred me on during the good days and through these challenging times.

Lastly, I owe all this to a wonderful lady, Joan Toggitt, who guided me on my long and wonderful career in the embroidery world, even long after she had left us. She was, and still is, my guardian angel.

Rosemary

Index

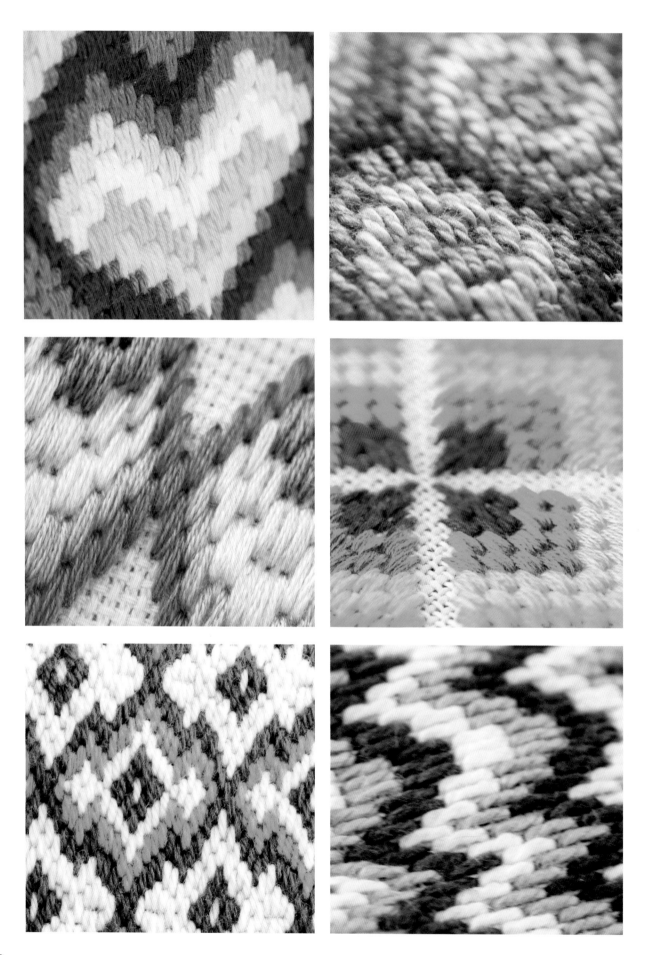

First published in 2023 by
Guild of Master Craftsman Publications Ltd Castle Place,
166 High Street, Lewes, East Sussex, BN7 1XU

Text © Rosemary Drysdale, 2023
Copyright in the Work © GMC Publications Ltd, 2023

ISBN 978-1-78494-646-3

All rights reserved.

The right of Rosemary Drysdale to be identified as the author of this work has been asserted in accordance with the Copyright, Designs and Patents Act 1988, sections 77 and 78.

No part of this publication may be reproduced, stored in a retrieval system or transmitted in any form or by any means without the prior permission of the publisher and copyright owner.

This book is sold subject to the condition that all designs are copyright and are not for commercial reproduction without the permission of the designer and copyright owner.

While every effort has been made to obtain permission from the copyright holders for all material used in this book, the publishers will be pleased to hear from anyone who has not been appropriately acknowledged and to make the correction in future reprints.

The publishers and author can accept no legal responsibility for any consequences arising from the application of information, advice or instructions given in this publication.

A catalogue record for this book is available from the British Library.

Senior Project Editor: Wendy Hobson
Managing Art Editor: Jennifer Stephens
Art Editor: Jacqui Crawford
Photographer: Sian Irvine & Quail Studio

Colour origination by GMC Reprographics
Printed and bound in China

To order a GMC book, contact:

GMC Publications Ltd
Castle Place, 166 High Street,
Lewes, East Sussex,
BN7 1XU
United Kingdom
Tel: +44 (0)1273 488005
www.gmcbooks.com